John Clark

The Works of the Caledonian Bards

Translated from the Galic. Volume I.

John Clark

The Works of the Caledonian Bards
Translated from the Galic. Volume I.

ISBN/EAN: 9783337329471

Printed in Europe, USA, Canada, Australia, Japan

Cover: Foto ©Thomas Meinert / pixelio.de

More available books at **www.hansebooks.com**

THE WORKS

OF THE

CALEDONIAN BARDS.

TRANSLATED FROM THE

GALIC.

VOLUME I.

EDINBURGH:
Printed for T. CADELL LONDON,
AND,
C. ELLIOT, EDINBURGH.

M,DCC,LXXVIII.

CONTENTS.

Preface Page	5
Introduction to the translations	21
Morduth, an antient heroic poem, book I.	29
———— book II.	49
———— book III.	73
The Chief of Scarlaw	80
The Chief of Feyglen	105
The Cave of Creyla	116
Culmala and Orwi	132
The Old Bard's Wish	141
Duchoil's Elegy	152
Sulvina's Elegy	159
Oran-Molla	164
The Words of Woe	174
The Approach of Summer	183
The Antient Chief	191

ERRATA.

ERRATA.

Page 64. line 20, *for* thou art at a beam, *read* thou art a beam.

Note to page 51. *for* Annals of Britain, *read* Annals of Scotland.

PREFACE.

A MIND, eager to examine the appearance of nature in her simplest garb, and sollicitous to contemplate the extent of her power, without the aid of art, must enjoy a rational pleasure from the poetical compositions of the Celtic bards. No set of men ever displayed greater knowledge of the avenues which lead directly to the heart. They first arrived at eminence, by the exertion of superior talents; and the industry with which they cultivated the human mind soon rendered the order venerable. They maintained their exalted station on principles, of which the voice of reason and philosophy most approve. They did not terrify weak minds into the belief of preposterous hypotheses, which they could not demonstrate, nor overawe the populace, by pretending to have intercourse with oracles, and being the favourites of any divinity. Their aim was to fill the minds of their hearers with great and liberal sentiments; to make them enamoured of heroism; and to inspire their hearts with that generous love to mankind, which constitutes the happiness and dignity of human nature.

Modern œconomy, however, seems to entertain a very different opinion of the merits of the bards, and represents them as a set of useless, lazy vagrants, who subsisted on the industry of others; and assures us, we have little reason to regret the extinction of their order. But this is not the only case where the voice of censure has advanced assertions in the face of facts, and directly opposite to the principles of fair reasoning.

The warmest advocates for the perfections of human nature, will readily allow, that the heart of man still requires some cultivation; and, although a proper field for nourishing, will not, of its own accord, produce certain plants. Conscious of this truth, mankind have, in all ages, contributed towards the support of individuals, who were supposed

posed to be wiser than the rest, for the purpose of improving the heart. These have generally extended their influence, not in proportion to their own abilities, but the weakness of their constituents; and few of them, like the Celtic bards, have lived up to the tenets they professed; for no instance can be found of one of these aspiring to wealth or power, but have, on all occasions, expressed the keenest contempt for every other gratification, but that of inspiring their patrons with magnanimity, and their countrymen with heroism. Living thus beyond the reach of corruption, their compositions are the genuine offspring of their untainted minds; and, though now dragged from their antient dignity, they have left monuments behind them, sufficient to proclaim their former splendor.

The common people in the Highlands of Scotland are, at this day, endowed with a poetical taste for nervous composition, far superior to that subsisting among the same class of men in any other nation of Europe,
with

with all the boasted refinements introduced by the propagation of learning in later ages Locked up for many centuries in an unfertile corner of an island, and, by the locality of their language, deprived of all intercourse with the rest of mankind, modern improvement can lay no claim to the establishment of this poetical taste. To account for it, by ascribing to the Highlanders talents superior to their southern brethren, might favour of rashness, presumption, and partiality; but, to attribute this advantage to the superiority of their language, is asserting, what I hope convincingly to prove, by occasional remarks annexed to these poems.

The majesty, and beautiful energy of the Galic, appear no where so conspicuous, as when a translation of the compositions it contains is attempted. While the original poems found among the Highlanders are rehearsing before us, the mind is captivated by the interesting scenes described. The subject is wrapped up in those thofe agreeable and pathetic terms, which dart, with irrefiftible force, upon the minds of the hearers. All the powers of attention are roufed. Every contemplating faculty is collected into one point, and rendered incapable to act on any fubject which is not immediately connected with the prefent fenfations of the heart. The mind, thus pre-engaged, is not at liberty to make a minute inquiry concerning the caufes from whence thefe agitations flow.

This is one reafon why the natives of the Highlands are high paffioned, rafh, and ungovernable in their tempers. The images of objects are painted in colours fo glowing, that, when difagreeable, the mind lofes all command. Even when a Highlandman has long refided in the low countries, early habit leads him to think in Galic; and, fuch is the energy and force of this language, that he often breaks out into a rage, at circumftances which appear perfectly trifling, when fpoken or conceived in Englifh. But, when a tranflator attempts to delineate thefe fentiments in any other language, he will find them ftripped of fo many comprehenfive terms, and poetical flowers, peculiar to the Galic, that the perufal of them muft be in danger of difgufting thofe who are acquainted with the originals.

The antient poems ftill extant in the Galic, exhibit a picture of the Caledonians fo different from that given them in hiftory, that one could fcarcely imagine them to be the fame people, if the manners and cuftoms alluded to in thefe poems did not fubfift at this day among the Highlanders. The tranfactions of the weftern nations, beyond a certain period, are wrapped up in a mifty veil, which the breath of modern criticifm has, in vain, endeavoured to expel. This cloud, however, was not altogether, as hath been generally imagined, a confequence of their being deftitute of the ufe of letters. This defect, though material, their language was amazingly calculated to fupply; and, had they not been crufhed by the
fuperior

superior cunning of aspiring tyrants, there is great reason to conclude, that the introduction of literature would have met with several oral registers kept with great exactness, by which their account of themselves might be traced back for an incredible space of time. The purity with which the poems of Ossian, Morguth, Deal, and many other bards, both in Scotland and Ireland, have been handed down to our own days, are sufficient to support the truth of this assertion.

The Celtic language was constructed on principles the best calculated for preserving as well as describing events. Every accent struck with such force upon the mind, that the memory had little trouble in retaining a composition of great length, and of rehearsing the same after the first or second hearing. Had this language then been cultivated with the same degree of industry that has been bestowed on others far less capable of answering the intended purposes, mankind might have enjoyed several advantages to which they are now strangers. The
drudgery

drudgery of the schools might have been performed with half the present labour, and the study of each science would have become more expeditious.

It is astonishing, that an event so remarkable as that of expelling the language of their ancestors, and adopting that of the Saxons, by the King and Court of Scotland, should be totally overlooked by the historians of that nation. It admits of no doubt, however, that this must have happened during the reign of Malcolm Canmore. He is the last king of Scotland whose name is significant in the Galic. All before him are so, as far as genuine history reaches. The influence of his Queen, Margaret, at a court where she herself was the chief ornament, was successfully exerted to render her language fashionable. The flower of the English, who had fled from the conqueror, shared the distresses, and now tasted the good fortunes of Margaret, could not fail of seconding these efforts. The Saxon language soon became general along the eastern coast of of Scotland; which lands, we are informed, Malcolm bestowed on the followers of his Queen. They stepped into the first offices in the kingdom, spread their own language among their domestics and adherents, and banished the Galic to the unfertile mountains, where it has hitherto maintained its existence with surprising fortitude, notwithstanding the various schemes, practised of late, for its final destruction.

We can advance nothing with certainty concerning what period many of the following poems have been composed. Had the Highlanders, like other nations, been accustomed to admit the religious opinions of the times into their works, modern inquiry might have been directed to form tolerable notions concerning the different æras in which their authors lived. But this never was, nor could, with propriety, be expected to be the case. When the Galic language was in the meridian of its splendor, the Christian religion was altogether unknown to the Celtic nations; and, since it hath been introduced amongst

mongſt them, their own language has been much on the decline. This accounts for the extreme meanneſs to which every poem, on religious ſubjects, ſinks in the Galic. Although a compoſer may be furniſhed in that language with a luxuriant richneſs of nervous expreſſions, when war, love, or paſtoral poetry is the theme, if he change it to religion, he will find his ſubject dreſſed in a garb of meanneſs, from which he will in vain endeavour to reſcue it by the moſt ſtrenuous exertion of all his powers. It is no wonder then, that bards of great parts have ſedulouſly avoided a ſubject, for which their language could furniſh them with no terms. So little mention is made of religion, that the poems compoſed before and after the introduction of Chriſtianity, are not to be diſtinguiſhed, except ſome pieces which have been compoſed during the two laſt centuries, which greatly partake of that narrowneſs of mind, and thoſe illiberal ſentiments which diſtinguiſh the enthuſiaſtical fanatics of theſe times, from whom the Highlanders borrowed ed such mean and contemptible notions of religion.

But, although the Celtic nations embraced the Romish religion, and adopted all their terms, as they had none of their own, still they were loath to relinquish their favourite FLATHINNIS, or *Happy Isle*, in the western sea, where the ghosts of their fathers were said to reside: 'Where,' says Morguth, 'the bright sun of heaven de-
' scends each night, in all the majesty of
' his flaming beauty, to chear the warriors
' of old. There he sits in his hall of splen-
' dor. No oaks burn within; no surly blast
' wanders without. The giver of the morn-
' ing warms all with his presence. The
' ghosts of our fathers hearken to his tale
' from the land of hills. By times they
' hear of their sons, and listen with ears of
' attention. Pleasant are the looks of the
' aged, when their children are mentioned
' with the sons of fame. But, when they
' fly from their foes, the souls of their fathers
' are sad; they hide their dim heads with
' shame,

'shame, and fly from the presence of the
'sun of heaven.'

Frequent descriptions of this nature seem to have realized in the minds of the Celtae this FLATHINNIS. No wonder, then, that they were reluctant to eraze from their breasts all remembrance of a place which their bards had taught them to consider as their eternal home. To be deprived of that happiness which fancy had promised them there, which the bards had described with a falacious kind of demonstration, entirely to resign all pretensions to that paradise, where the ghosts of their fathers were supposed to have gone before them, was not consistent with that paternal fondness which the human mind has, in all ages, discovered for the first principles which superstition imprints on the heart. Heaven, as described by the first propagators of Christianity, they imagined, corresponded, in several respects, with their own FLATHINNIS; and it is reported by tradition, that they would listen to no accounts of any other place of happiness

happiness than that in which they were informed their fathers resided. However that be, it is certain, that heaven has no other name in the Galic to this day, than that of this imaginary island; and, what renders this the more remarkable, there is perhaps no other term respecting religion, in the Galic, that is not literally borrowed from some other language.

It was proposed at first to enter more minutely into a comparison of both languages in the notes; but several gentlemen objected to the inserting any part of the original, as useless to the English reader, for whose benefit alone this work was published. At their desire, therefore, these critical remarks will be annexed to the originals of these poems, which it is proposed to publish soon, as some of these pieces have been collected from the mouths of persons now living in the Highlands, and have not yet been printed in the Galic, owing principally to the small demand for books in that dialect.

The

The present translation was undertaken, with a view to rescue from the ruins of a perishing language, some of those poems which have met with universal applause from the people for whose use they were composed. To these the British nation is indebted for that martial spirit, which the inhabitants of that part of the island have displayed in many of her contests. The Galic bards uniformly inculcate two material principles in the human heart; Never to forsake a friend, nor fear a foe.

Those who are acquainted with the originals, will no doubt be surprised that the translator has passed over compositions of greater merit than those inserted in this volume. But, as he has often been compleatly mortified, on comparing his own versions with the originals, he was desirous of knowing the judgment of the public concerning his manner of executing these translations. If he shall be so happy as to meet with their approbation, he will proceed with more spirit to the translation of those poems of a loftier nature. But, if their sentiments shall coincide with his own, in considering them as inimitable in an English version, he will readily desist from the undertaking, and rest satisfied with having exerted every effort in his power, in vain, to rescue from oblivion the venerable compositions of the CALEDONIAN BARDS.

INTRODUCTION.

HAIL, oral offspring of the human breath,
  Smooth piercing accents, gift of bounteous heav'n!
Without thy friendly aid the breast of man
Would burst with the big load of fetter'd thought.
Nor voice of tale could e'er salute his ear,
Nor song historic fraught with warlike deeds.
The fertile bosom of the heavenly bard
Had been the parent and the grave of songs.
Mens sons had never heard the deeds of old;
Nor wish'd to live in breath of midnight tale.
Had the tongue mutely roll'd within his mouth,
Man's life, insipid, had unnotic'd pass'd,
And been to non-existence much allied.

Then, to the first of Powers, whose mighty art
Establish'd commerce 'twixt the heart and tongue;
To Him, who, from the feeble force of sound,
Brought accents piercing as the pointed steel;
Who form'd the tongue obedient to the will,
Be the first offspring of that Will addrest.

Fir'd with the greatness of the liberal gift,
Which he enjoys above the other sons
Of nature, who traverse the spreading fields,

INTRODUCTION.

The grateful of the race of man shall bend,
In adoration bow the knee to HIM,
From whom the riches of all bounty flow.
 Yet, thou penurious, mercenary son
Of narrow soul! my words seem strange to thee.
Thou never felt one animating ray
Of gratitude to HIM who cloath'd the fields,
And fill'd the waves with riches for thy use.
Thy darken'd soul no harmony can reach.
On thee the sun-beams roll in vain at noon.
His strength, his kindness, he exerts in vain,
To thaw the feelings of thy frozen heart.—
Thou miscreant! stop the venom of thy breath,
Nor frown so surly on my simple song.
Its fire attempts not to dissolve thy breast.
Listen not to themes you cannot understand,
Nor censure sentiments you never knew.
 But thou, O feeling heart, sweet plant of light!
Image of HIM to whom the nations kneel!
To thee, with reverence, I address my song:
To thee I look with expectation's eye,
And earnest wish for approbation's nod;
And where thy purer breath shall mark me wrong,
I'll stand corrected, and receive my doom.
 If thus, divided in their various minds,

INTRODUCTION.

The different hearers of my tale should stand;
The frowns of one as earnest I desire,
As I petition for the other's smile.——
   O thou eternal Parent of all pow'r!
Who will'd to being thy unnumber'd worlds,
Who but thyself can show the hidden springs
From which the meanest of thy works proceeds?
Reflecting man, with admiration, feels
His pow'r to publish, or conceal his thoughts.
The organs which perform this wond'rous task,
In close attendance wait upon his will.
His words the hearers ear uninjur'd pierce,
And tell his breast the purport of their flight.
The pow'r of sound, an unexhausted source!
Has furnish'd various languages for man.
These all address the heart in diff'rent tones,
As nations varied under which they grew.
One breathes majestic in a Homer's song,
And draws the battle like the painter's brush.
Virgil, with art, has dress'd another's brow
With flowers, whose blooming lustre ne'er shall
    fade.
And thou, O Mother of the Galic muse!
Have I injur'd thee, thus to name thee last?
Perhaps I have; and, wert thou known like these,
                         My

My want of judgment had been juftly blam'd.
  But fay, thou parent of the Celtic fong!
How comes thy beauties thus to lie conceal'd?
Has no fweet, bold, poetic fon of thine,
Held forth thy richnefs in luxuriant ftrains?
Haft thou in vain difplay'd thy breaft, adorn'd
With the inviting charms of rhet'ric's pow'r;
And has thy children, of perception void,
With ftupid looks beheld thee thus unmov'd?
  Interrogation's words are juft and ftrong;
But feeble are the anfwers we can make.
In vain, alas! we tell the ftranger's fons,
Whofe eyes cannot behold thy dazzling light,
That bards have fung, and hearers dropt a tear,
As the fong pierc'd into the hardeft heart:
That gloomy brows have foften'd at the found;
Infenfibility has fled, and left
The nobleft paffions ruling in the heart.
  Thus we, in vain attempt, in borrowed words,
To draw afide the veil that keeps thee hid,
And fhew thee to admiring eyes, array'd
In beauty, ftrength, and majefty fublime.
But thou our efforts baffles all with fcorn,
And frowns feverely on the foolifh bard,
Who ftrives to drefs thee in another garb.
                                    She,

She, whom the feeble song thus serenades,
Was once admir'd, and spoke by nations great.
Inspir'd by her sweet notes, great chiefs and kings
Gain'd fame immortal in the Celtic states.
Her breath gave laws to Europe's spacious plains.
Beneath her spreading wings, a martial race!
The warlike sons of Gaul were known to fame.
In time her multiplying tribes encreas'd;
Too great their bulk for continental bounds.
Then rais'd our fathers, with adventu'rous hand,
The spreading sail, and seiz'd the passing blast,
By whose impetuous breath, with flying speed,
They pass'd the high-swell'd bosom of the waves
To Britain's isle. With liberty they rang'd
Along th' extended plains, and rising brows
Of hills, that rudely rear their lofty heads
Above the dusky clouds of sailing mist,
That travel round the sea-girt, cliffy coast.
There flourish'd long, before the scribing art
Was known, to place their deeds upon record.
Before them Nature spread, with liberal hands,
The choicest riches of the annual crop.
Man tasted, unrestrain'd by pride or pow'r,
The blessings which were giv'n for him to know.
                                        Such

Such was the case, e'er property assum'd
Her selfish claim to all the fertile plains,
Which heav'n had granted for the use of man.

O fatal foe to human nature's race!
Destructive gratitude! that first taught men
To bend, with reverence, to the worthless son
Of him who glow'd with patriotic zeal!
In vain they hop'd the father's worth would live,
And rashly plac'd him on the seat of pow'r.—
Deluded croud! your offspring long shall mourn,
In bonds and misery, the hasty deed:
Tyrannic chiefs will wield oppression's rod,
And your sons sink beneath that pow'r you gave.

Fain would the struggling efforts of the bard
Pursue a theme more smooth, less hostile words,
And, in persuasive accents, raise the song
To those whose several beauties fire his breast.—

Daughters of Babel! by whose oral aid
The numerous sons of Adam have convey'd
Their inward feelings, whether real or forg'd,
Thro' various organs to the kindred mind:
Think not I aim to sing, with breath profane,
In strains detractive of the high renown
Of you, bright messengers of mutual thought,
Whose never absent help conveys, with speed,

Each

Each various wish, with ease from breast to breast.
One of your number has experienc'd woe,
And struggl'd long beneath the frowns of fate.
Dragg'd from her antient greatness, now she lurks
In cliffy corners of the British isles.
If beauty in distress should urge my sigh,
Or warm my breast beyond permitted bounds,
Think not your merit has unnotic'd pass'd:
My eyes are open also to your charms.

    Come, ghosts of bards, who sung among the heath
Of Morven's woody hills, on Albian shore!
Say, whether would you wish your song to fall,
And walk majestic to the arms of death,
Array'd in beauty, elegance, and strength;
Or, would you condescend to have it stript
Of that sublimity in which it shines,
And, drest in mean attire, a simple tale
Depriv'd of numbers, energy, and sound,
Permit its import to be told to those,
Who cannot view it in its pristine state?

    Consent, great shades! and I, with sacred awe,
Will look into the treasures ye have left,
Mourn as I view that height I cannot reach,
And sigh those beauties which I cannot tell.
                                      Come,

INTRODUCTION.

Come, then, Britannia's voice of modern days!
Come, and, with generous frankneſs known to few,
Aſſiſt, while in thy mirror I diſplay,
And trace the beauties of thy rival's face;
That men may know the conqueſt thou haſt made,
And view her ſtrength who ſank beneath thy arm.
Not ſmall the vict'ry—heavenly were her charms!
And tho' ſhe fell, ſhe juſtly claims a tear.

MORDUTH.

MORDUTH*,

AN ANTIENT

HEROIC POEM.

IN THREE BOOKS.

BOOK I.

ART thou on the wings of thy speed, O wind? Doſt thou travel with all thy ſtrength? Come in mildneſs to the cave of my reſt, O breath of the north! My ſtrength is
with

---

* The accounts which tradition gives of the author of this poem, are various. Some aſſert that he was a chief, whoſe territories lay to the north of the Grampian hills, towards the eaſtern coaſt. Others affirm, that he was bard to Morduth, King of the Caledonians. Another party maintain, that he was family-bard to the unfortunate houſe of Dunairm, whoſe hiſtory he has introduced into the preſent poem. But, although they differ in their accounts of his ſtation, they all agree that his name was Donthal; and the induſtry with which his compoſitions have been handed down, are ſufficient to ſhow the veneration which they entertain for his memory.

with the years that have flown: My friends are with the tenants of the tomb. I sit lonely in my cave of woe, in the days of my feeble years. Leave thy wrathful storms behind thee, when thou rollest over my rocks, thou hasty blast!

My speed on the hills was once like thine, O wind! my strength as the rocks of Cruival. The ghosts of my foes wander on many hills: The marks of my steel is in many battles. But thou, perhaps, like me, wilt some time mourn thy departed strength, and wander with slow steps on the hills. Thou wilt then in vain endeavour to drive thy hundred clouds before thee. The forest that now bends at thy approach, will laugh, when thou desirest the haughty oaks to bow their branchy heads before thee. Even the feeble heath will scorn thy strength. Come, then, in friendship to my gray hairs, O wind; for the days of thy own feeble years approach.

Lay down the bow, and kindle the oaks, hunter of Corri; * the course of night is towards

* Corri is one of the many significant terms in the Galic

wards us. The sun trembles in the west. The
isle of his sleep † has three times opened wide
its gates, and cried, ' Come in all thy flaming
' beauty, O sun !'

The

tion. Concavities of one or two miles in diameter, are
frequently to be seen in the face of some large ranges of
mountains. The springs which issue from three sides of
this concavity, always meet about the center, where the
junction of so many rivulets forms a little stream, which is
afterwards joined by other rivulets from both sides, till it
arrives at the bottom of the mountains from which it col-
lects the waters. Then the hollow through which the river
passes, is called a *Glen*. But the face of the hills, to
which it owes its birth, is called *Corri*.

† The sun was supposed to sleep in Flathinnis; or, *the
Isle of Peace*, in the western ocean. As nature rejoices or
grieves according as this celestial body bestows or with-
holds its smiles; an ambition of which the human mind
seems, in no age, to be defective, induced the Celtæ to
send the ghosts of their departed friends to this imaginary
paradise. To make HERE happy, by reflecting on the
prospect of HEREAFTER, is a consolation at which man-
kind have eagerly grasped, in all ages and nations. Va-
rious are the appearances under which the imagination has
represented this happiness. But, when the most perfect de-
lineations of it are minutely examined, well may we ex-
claim at the end, ' 'Tis but to know how little can be
known.'—Tho' we have, at last, obtained an infal-

lible

The clouds of night hide their dark heads behind the eastern hills. By times they look forth from their hidden caves, and watch the departure of the broad-faced king of the sky. Put on your wings of speed, ye clouds, and come forth. The ghosts of a hundred heroes prepare a bed for your bright * foe in the Isle of Peace.

Blest

---

sible system of religion, and have as much communicated to us as was judged proper or necessary for us to know, occasional inquiries into the notions of our ancestors, on so interesting a subject, will not, perhaps, be deemed altogether impertinent. These inquiries, at this distance of time, cannot be expected to be altogether satisfactory. The glimmering light by which they are directed, is only to be gathered from the remains of antient poetry, which consists rather in allusions to, than any descriptions of religion, as the bards never wrote professedly on that subject.

* The sun is frequently called the *Foe of Night* in antient poetry. The joy which the ghosts, in this imaginary isle, were said to express, when he descended from the sky, shewed a great extent of imagination. It was supposed that the ghosts of the most courageous warriors sat next him; but those who had been cowards in their lifetime, were kept at the extremities of the island. We do not, however, hear of any other punishment inflicted on them, than that of being kept at a distance from the sun.

The

Bleſt be the fair maid of thy love, O hunter;
unerring be the arrow of thy bow! Thou com-
forteſt

The Highlanders, accuſtomed to hear the bold, lofty, and elegant compoſitions of their bards on this ſubject, were not a little aſtoniſhed, about the beginning of the preſent century, when one of thoſe popular preachers, who are ſaid to have reformed mankind, attempted to eſtabliſh a very different hypotheſis; and poſitively affirmed, in a ſermon, that the ſun was the place mentioned in ſcripture, as appointed for the reception of the damned.

When the common people in the north are any ways puzzled about ſeeming improprieties, in matters of religion, ſome of their reſpectable teachers ſent them from the ſouth, find a very ſhort, but ſubſtantial ſolution to ſuch difficulties. They ſometimes tell theſe people, that their ignorance, and want of penetration, is the reaſon which makes it appear ſo to them. That theſe matters have been minutely examined by the wiſe part of mankind, who have all agreed in it; and that they themſelves are the only perſons in the world who entertain a doubt of it. That the reſt of mankind, in compaſſion to their ignorance, have raiſed an immenſe ſum of money, to be applied for the purpoſe of opening their eyes; and conclude, with complimenting themſelves, as the favourite veſſels choſen to put theſe pious reſolutions in execution.

That an immenſe ſum was raiſed for this laudable purpoſe, is a fact which every native of that country will acknowledge, with the warmeſt overflowings of gratitude.

But

forteſt me in my tottering age.—But ſit thou down in my cave, and let the rocks contend with the wind. I will tell thee of warriors who are now no more; of heroes who ſleep within the ſilent tomb.

Pleaſant

But the offended feelings of the more penetrating part of them are juſtly rouſed, when they reflect, that this money is applied to purpoſes very different from thoſe intended by the generous donors.

That the ſuppreſſion of vice, and promotion of virtue, is the aim of the *Society for propagating Chriſtian Knowledge, &c.* can admit of no doubt. That they have proved themſelves deſtitute of abilities to put their good intention in execution, is an aſſertion, which, I am ſorry to ſay, is ſupported by truth. Theſe gentlemen ſeem to have entertained ſtrange notions of the Highlanders. They imagined that the moſt ignorant men whom they could collect from the dregs of the people, well enough qualified to eſtabliſh any ſyſtem of religion among the mountaineers. Magnifying their own conſequence, and entertaining an unſufferable degree of contempt for the intellects of the people they were about to reform, they have rendered themſelves ridiculous to the intelligent part of mankind, and injured the cauſe they meant to advance. The converts to the Roman Catholic perſuaſion, are becoming every day more numerous. The reaſon is obvious. Their prieſts are all men of a liberal education, and generally of extenſive knowledge. Men, verſed in all the ſophiſtry of argumentation,

Pleasant are the thoughts of former times; sweet the remembrance of the days that have fled. Return, ye deeds of my youth, and let my soul yet behold the years of my strength. Let the battles of other times roll before me; and let me view the steel of heroes who have been.

Bend

argumentation, will find little difficulty in refuting a doctrine supported by a parcel of weavers, shoemakers, &c. who, being too lazy to work at their own trades, have taken it into their heads to reform a people already wise, acute, and penetrating, far beyond themselves. As these servants of the Society have no knowledge of science or literature, they generally endeavour to swell themselves in the eyes of the populace, by groans, sighs, and other marks of hypocrisy. A species of imposition, and an insult offered to the Author of all religion, for which every man of genuine piety must express the warmest indignation!

If we look back into the history of Scotland for the last two centuries, we will find every passage filled with human miseries, created by a similar set of men, on a similar subject. The people of the low countries are now recovered from their dream. Would it not be an object worthy the attention of the Legislature, to prevent such an infection spreading in the Highlands, by sending men of parts and learning to instruct them?

Bend forward your awful presence from the clouds of your rest, warriors of old! ye who raise no more the spear in battles, be near. Your sons shall hear of your strength; and a tear will trickle down their cheeks when they pass by the narrow dwelling of the mighty.

A tale of other years rushes on my soul. I remember the deeds of the days that are past.

Gloomy was the night; for the moon hid her fair face from the storm. The stars lay asleep among the folds of their dark clouds. Winds and seas came in haste from other lands. The battles of rocks and storms were terrible, when the ghost of Salmor * came forth from his watery bed in the womb of ocean. His footsteps were on the frothy wings of the troubled

---

* The poems concerning this Salmor are now lost; but tradition makes frequent mention of him. He was drowned, in passing from the continent of Scotland to his own house, in one of the Hebrides, on hearing that his wife was taken prisoner, and his lands laid waste by Tuthmar, a chief of Norway, whose father Salmor is said to have killed in battle. A beautiful poem is said to have been composed by Salmor's bard, on this subject; but the translator has not been so lucky as to meet with it.

troubled waves. The gathering of the whirlwind was there: The son of the grave rose on the wings of the blast. He stood on Craigduth's cliffy brow. The course of the storm was round the trembling of his pointless spear. He leaned forward from his bed of clouds, and his words were heard.

Raise, chiefs of Albin *, raise the spears of your strength. Let the voice of shields be heard,

* Albin, which signifies a *mountainous country*, seems once to have been the name of all the island, as well as Britain, in the Galic. But, after the Saxons had defeated the South-Britons, and become masters of that division, their part received the name of *Saffon*, the latter *x* being neither written nor pronounced in the Galic. Such of the South-Britains as maintained their independency, were honoured with the appellation of *Ualsh*, or *Nobility*, in opposition to the vulgar who submitted to the conquerors; and the northern division, comprehending all Scotland, has ever since been invariably known in the Galic by the name of ALBIN.

To launch forth into the rugged paths of controversy, is beyond the limits or intention of the present notes: But, when the definitions which truth compells the translator to subjoin to these poems, are directly opposite to the assertions of writers of reputation on the same subject, a vindication of them becomes necessary.

heard, and the gathering of warriors be seen. Not feeble is the arm of the coming foe. The rolling

The Rev. Mr Whitaker, in a recent history of the antient Britains, has displayed the knowledge of a man of science, and the liberality of a gentleman, in a manner which is seldom to be met with in the productions of those who professedly write to injure the reputation of an individual, or the antiquity of a people. It is with reluctance, therefore, I proceed to refute the assertions of an author, endowed with many qualifications to command respect. But, since he has ventured to publish as facts, what is directly opposite to this definition, it becomes necessary to examine how far he is countenanced by truth; as it would be dangerous to lay any fact before the public as genuine, while an author of Mr Whitaker's shining abilities stands unconquered in the field to oppose it.

As the Galic is at present little known, and less studied, ignorance concerning any matter wrapped up within the folds of its garment, would very improperly be attributed as a defect to any writer of character in the republic of letters. But, since Mr Whitaker has, of his own accord, started the contest, and plumed himself on an ideal conquest obtained over all the critics that ever wrote concerning that language, to examine his pretensions to merit, on a subject which he himself has chosen, will certainly be considered as no injustice.

Had Mr Whitaker mentioned the matter in words which could admit of any signification but one, his readers

rolling of Lochlin's dark ſhips is on the reſt-
leſs boſom of the waves.—Riſe, ſons of Albin,
rife,

ers would be apt to ſuſpect their own want of penetration, rather than imagine ſo great a man capable of writing ſuch abſurdities. I ſhall give the paſſage at large, as it will, no doubt, aſtoniſh every reader acquainted with the antient language of Britain, who has not already peruſed it.

'The whole body of the Caledonians, however, could never have been, and are not now denominated Albanich. The name of Caledonia, compriſing all that peninſula *of land* which lies to the north of the Friths, the appellation of Alban, or the mountains, could have been given *only* to the hilly part of the country, in oppoſitions to the levels of the eaſtern coaſt, and the plains immediately to the north of *Antoninus*'s Vallum. The inhabitants of theſe, I have already ſhown to have been denominated Mæatæ, or Lowlanders, by the Britons and Romans, and the inhabitants of the hills only, are denominated Albanich at PRESENT. The tribes of the Caledonian lowlands were denominated Mæatæ formerly, in contradiſtinction to the nations of the hills. And the clans of the Caledonian mountains are denominated Albanich at preſent, in oppoſition to the reſidenters of the lowlands.' *Whitaker's Genuine Hiſtory of the Britons*, page 270.

The Iriſh extraction of the Caledonians is a favourite hypotheſis of Mr Whitaker. The preſent extract is an
attempt

rise, and let the shields of your fathers meet the approaching foe. The attempt to establish it. Conscious, however, that the name of the country and inhabitants were against him, he endeavours to wave objections too stubborn to be conquered, by confining this name to a very inconsiderable part of the Caledonians, the mountaineers, that he might have the pleasure of mortifying the inhabitants of the low countries, by making their progenitors consist of a despicable colony from Ireland, whom he represents as subduing the Caledonians, and becoming masters of their country.

Since Mr Whitaker has thus deprived the most respectable part of the Caledonians of the only name by which they have been distinguished, in their antient language, for ages, far beyond the reach of history, it is to be wished, he had informed us under what denomination to class them for the future, whether with the Saxons or the Welsh; as the inhabitants of Britain have, for many centuries, had no other general distinction in the Galic than Albinich, Calsh, and Saffonich.

Had Mr Whitaker insisted on what happened in former ages only, references to history might be requisite to refute his assertions. But, since he has brought the subject to the present times, the controversy may be speedily and effectually decided. The reader may, if he pleases, ask any plebeian, who understands the Galic the signification of *Albinich*; he will readily receive for answer, that it is applied to all

The departure of the pale-fac'd son of night was on the wings of the sudden blast. Oaks of strength trembled before the haste of his retiring steps. The groans of the woods were heard,

all the inhabitants of Scotland, comprehending both those of the high and low countries. If he thinks his informer mistaken, he may put the same question to five hundred; they will all answer in the same words.—What a pity that Mr Whitaker had not consulted some of them, and not exposed his ignorance of a language, on the radical words of which he attempts to establish a groundless hypothesis; and from whose significant terms he endeavours to deduce the origin of nations.

Who can help regreting, that an author of Mr Whitaker's taste, elegance, extensive knowledge, and acute penetration, should suffer himself to become the dupe of prejudice, so far as to let himself thus be made an easy prey by every little critic, without putting them to the trouble of arranging arguments against him. No wonder that Cæsar and Tacitus have given such imperfect accounts of the Caledonians eighteen hundred years ago, since an antiquarian of Mr Whitaker's penetration, is entirely ignorant of the very name by which they are distinguished at this day.

As the inhabitants of Albin are the principal actors in the subsequent poems, this inquiry into the extent of their territories, became in some degree necessary.

heard, as he rushed on the clouds of his speed through their whistling locks.

Call my heroes from the chace, said the Chief of Albin's chiefs. Kindle my oaks on Drumfina *, that the blaze of many hills may gather my people from their hundred glens.

Such were the words of Morduth †, king of many straths, when his shield spoke the words of alarm. The sons of battle heard, and

---

* Of Drum, *a height*, and Fina, *heroes*. If we might presume, at this distance of time, to form conjectures concerning the scene of the present poem, we would be apt to place it in the north-east corner of Fife. There is to be seen, at this day, the remains of a fortification on the top of a hill, called *Drumcarro*, three miles west from St Andrew's. The country people, who always entertain gigantic notions of antient heroes, distinguish it at present by the name of the *Giant's Castle*. Though not high, it commands an extensive prospect along the eastern coast, from Lothian to near Aberdeen; and, therefore, a very proper situation for kindling a fire, according to the custom of the Scots, as a beacon to alarm the country, on the appearance of an enemy.

† Mor-duth, *great, dark hero*.—All the names in the Highlands, and most of the antient ones in the low countries,

and their swords forsook their dark dwellings in the sheath.

Morning shook her gray locks in the east, and bade the storm depart. The sun came forth in mildness from the waves, and his rising beams smiled on the blue steel of many heroes.

Caivglas * came forward with his cloud of strength. Many spears glittered behind Canard. Tommore of the massy shield gathered his warriors; and why should Mordale, the chief of the weighty steel, be last? His steps were foremost to meet the foes of Albin.

Who hath seen Swanar, said Caivglas, of other years?—are his warriors many?—I have met him in battle in the days of my strength; but other warriors now raise the spears of Albin.

Then they shall raise them in vain, said the son of Corvi. Swanar advances with the strength

---

countries, are at this day significant in the Galic; as Balfour, *cold town*; Lesly, *the half of the plain*; Somerville, *the man of weighty words*, &c.

* Chaibh-glas, *gray locks*;—Chean-ard, *high-head*;—Tom-more, *great hill*;—Mor-dale, *extended valley.*

strength of thousands. The dazzling beams of the sun sparkle round the gloss of his burnished armour. Tall warriors sink by his sides. Lofty trees seem little as he passeth. The rocks of Tirmore diminish beneath his extended stride. Terrible is the coming of Lochlin's * king! Who of Albin's race shall meet the strength of his arm?

Fly to thy cave of safety with all thy terrors, thou chief of the feeble arm, said Caivglas. Thy little soul trembles at the sound of danger, like the green leaf which shakes on a twig before the wind. Fly thou, like it, from the breath of winter; but here are oaks of strength, who have withstood the wrath of other storms. Has not the north poured all its fury on our land in the days of former years, and have we not met the blast unshaken?— Fly, thou warrior of yesterday, to the dwellings of little men.

---

* All the northern nations who invaded the Caledonians, were comprised under the general name of Lochlin, in the Galic, comprehending all the different states of Scandinavia. This name seems to have been given them by the Caledonians themselves; as the word, in their language, literally signifies, *The descendants of the ocean.*

Had he, who is but of yesterday, no foes but thee, well might he tremble for the fame of his battles:—But Lochlin's race shall meet his sword warm from thy side. Thy words have already been heard,—son of pride:—shew thy steel.

The spears of the two chiefs rose. Their warriors on either side half unsheathed. Now would the steel of Albin have pierced her own bosom, and fought the battle for Lochlin's race, had not the king, the shield of his people, come forward, and stopped the uplifted spear. He saw, with grief, the strife of the heroes. His frowning eye rolled from chief to chief. He dreaded the fall of his people, and his words were heard.—

Unsheath not the sword, ye sons of ocean, lest the tales of your land say we sank by your strength. Your fathers have often raised the spears in vain. Their tombs are many on our coasts; but smile, ye sons of the sea, for Albin has unsheathed the sword against herself.

Abashed, the sons of discord shrunk from the wrath of the king, like two dark clouds that roll their courſe to different hills, when the ſun looks forth in all his majeſty.—The vallies before them are ſad, and ſee the coming of the tear of heaven. Little hills are paſt unheeded.—Their courſe is towards the higheſt mountains, that rear their haughty heads in the wide extended regions of the ſky. —So dark, ſo tremenduous, rolled the chiefs their threatening courſe towards the foe.

The King came forward with the ſtrength of Albin, like the rock of Tonmore *, when it collects the force of all its cliffy brows to meet the boiſterous waves of ocean.

Swanar advanced with all his pointed ſpears. The ſtrength of Lochlin moved like a ſtorm from the north, which ſlowly rolls its clouds along the hills. No angry wind travels in wrath: No raſh blaſt wanders alone.—The ſtrength of the north blows equal.

The ſpears of Albin roſe high. The words of ſteel were heard. As the meeting of two great rocks in the bottom of the hollow glen, rolling with fury from the lofty brows of oppoſite

* Tonn-more, *great waves.*

posite hills, when the brown hind flies with horror the danger of their course; so bold, so fierce, so terrible, was the meeting of the two hosts. Many foes sank before the strength of Albin. Many more supplied the places of the fallen.

The horror of battle roared along the heath. Mordale strode among the slain. A bloody stream pours from Canard's spear. The soul of each hero was bright; but who could withstand the strength of thousands?

Morduth saw the backward steps of his people, and the kindling rage of his mighty soul awaked. He raised his terrible spear in wrath, and the groans of new-formed ghosts were heard. But his heroes were distant far, and his foes were many. He retired at last to his host, like the angry torrent, when, murmuring, it falls from the shaggy brow of the rock. An hundred times the pride of ocean bids his furious waves climb the rugged height. An hundred times the rock throws them back into the restless deep. The voice of their rage is terrible, as they shake their hoary locks to the wind.

Why

Why doeft thou frown in the weft, fair haired traveller of the fky? Our foes were not of the feeble. Often have the dark clouds concealed thy own beauty in the day of the ftorm. But, when thou driveft the wind from thy lands, and purfueft the tempeft from thy fields; when the clouds vanifh at thy nod, and the whirlwind lies ftill at thy defire; when thou lookeft down in triumph on our land, and fhakeft the white locks of thy awful majefty, in pride, above our hills; when we behold thee clothed in all thy lovelinefs, we rejoice in the conqueft thou haft made in heaven, and blefs thy friendly beams, O Sun!——

But retire to thy heathy bed with fmiles, bright monarch of the fky; for we will yet be renowned.

MORDUTH,

THRICE had the dark-haired night shook her misty wings in the east. Thrice had the trembling stars attempted to look forth. Thrice had the sighs of the vanquished mingled with the wind, when the ghosts of departed heroes were seen stalking in wrathful steps on the hills. Meteors rolled together on the heath. Feeble voices whispered in the clouds. The affrighted host heard it, and dreaded the frown of their fathers who never fled.

The king stood on Ardcraig's * brow. An hundred spears are half erected round. Each spear supports the grief of a chief. Behind stood the darkened host, a gloomy cloud! The looks of the king were round him to behold their thoughts, and his words came forth.

Fate

* Ard-craig, *high rock.*

Fate frowns, and the feeble retire from danger. The voice of the storm is heard, and the sons of little men fly to the cottage; but the rock meets the breath of the north, and shakes not. The course of the storm is abroad; but oaks of strength raise their heads regardless of its wrath.

Say, then, chiefs, are we of the sons of little men? Are our spears feeble twigs sprung from Albin's oaks of strength?

The force of many foes rushed from the north in the days of other years. Did our fathers fly before them?—No, warriors! they fled not from the strength of thousands Their spears rose high: The sons of the sea sank before them. Shall we then fly on the hills of their triumph, where the ghosts of the foe were wont to murmur from the whirlwind as they fled from tomb to tomb?—These gray stones, the marks of other battles, lift their mossy heads in the face of heaven, and seem to say, ' Your fathers fled not.'

The king spoke. The chiefs stood fixed in grief. By times they viewed their spears, and grasped their bossy shields. Swords were half-unsheathed,

unsheathed, and half-formed accents mingled with the wind.

Morcan *, the leader of Aulduth's † warriors, came forward. Thrice he shook the locks of his age. Thrice his spear is dashed against an oak. His eye dropt the tear of woe; his mouth the words of grief.

My name, O king! was not wont to be mentioned with the feeble. I was not accustomed to fly before my foes. Part of my strength has fled with my years; but fear has not yet found room in my withered nerves. The hope of my gray hairs was in the rising fame of my son. His hand, I thought, would raise my tomb. Nor spear, nor tomb, shall ever rise by him. He rushed forward in the battle,

---

* Mor-chean, *great head*.—This distinction was not altogether so rude as the elegant author of the Annals of Britain affirms, in the etymology of the name of Malcolm Canmore. The idea of loftiness, as well as greatness, is expressed by the original; and, therefore, very properly applied to a man exalted above the common people, whether by stature or station.

† Auld-dath, *black-stream*.

battle, where no friend could aid. The rising of many spears was round him:—He sank in the midst of falling foes.

Peace to the shade of the hero, said the king! he must not wander alone to the misty dwellings of his fathers; some chief of Albin must attend. The land of clouds is gloomy. The warrior is a stranger, and alone.

*Ogvan, the son of Corvi, grasped his shield, and shook his spear to the wind.—Shall we rest till morning show her fair face in the east; or raise the steel among the clouds of night, and lay the foe with the deer of their feast?

Often, said Canard, did our fathers give the shell of joy; but when did they spread death round the feast of strangers?—The mighty are among the race of Lochlin. We too will rejoice in our turn; or, if we fall, let us not depart, like the dim cloud that travels over the mountains, while the moon is asleep, and the twinkling stars shrink from the presence of the storm. The morning will soon shake her gray locks in the east. The sun will look

forth

---

* Og-bhan, *young fair warrior.*—

forth from the blue fields of his pride, and smile on the raising of our steel, while death frowns grimly at the point of each spear.

Let heroes who expect their tombs to rise by the white-armed daughters of beauty, said the bearer of Dunairm's * shield, rest till morning; but Moralt shall fall amid the shades of night. No tomb of mine shall rise: No tear from the lovely shall bathe it. None shall lament over me, saying, ' Oh my hero!'— None shall lament over me, saying, ' Oh my son!' † My arrow hath pierced the breast of the lovely: My spear is stained with the blood of my kindred.

My fathers were the foes of Albin. Their spears rose with Lochlin's king. I longed to travel upon the waves of ocean. Six warriors raised my white sails. The wind came in haste from the north: Waves gathered strength from the blast. Seas mingled with clouds

that

---

* Dunairm, *the tower of arms.*

† ' They shall not lament for him, saying, ah my brother, or ah sister! They shall not lament for him, saying, ah lord, or ah his glory! He shall be buried with the burial of an ass, drawn and cast forth beyond the gates of Jerusalem.' Jerem. xxii. 18.

that hurried along the face of the deep. The high hills of Albin rose on the top of the waves *. The green woods of Sliavan shook their

* What is here translated, *The high hills, &c.* stands in the original Dheirich Albin air braidh-tonn. The Dh in the first word having the sound of y in English; and in the middle of the last, being, according to the genius of the Celtic language, quiescent, is pronounced thus: Yeirich Albin air braitoin; Brai signifying invariably *top*, and toin *waves*.

To pretend to give a definition of the word *Britain* just, and, at the same time, different from all that have already been advanced by so many eminent writers on that subject, would bespeak a degree of arrogance which the Translator would sedulously wish to avoid: But, he has the greatest reason to believe, that the etymology of it cannot, with propriety, be deduced from any other root than *Brai-toin*.

That the language of the Gauls and Britons was the same, we learn from undoubted authority; and, it would be doing material injustice to the intelligent reader, to imagine him capable of supposing this could be any other than the Celtic. As this was undoubtedly the first language spoke on both sides of the English channel, it renders it more than probable, that it is the only one in which the origin of the word *Britain* is to be found.

That Britain was at first peopled from the opposite coast of Gaul, is a rational hypothesis; and accordingly has been

their locks before the bounding of our bark.
The hall of Dunairm was the home of
strangers. The gray haired chief stretched
forth

been adopted by the most eminent historians; That, as Britain was within sight of Gaul, the inhabitants would bestow on it some name before they crossed the channel, is a supposition not altogether improbable. The Celtic language contains no names that are not significant of the external appearance of the objects on which they are bestowed. Ingenuity could certainly suggest no term more significant of the appearance of Britain from France, viewing it over the convexity which the globe forms in the breadth of the channel, than, ' The land on the top of the waves.' The antient poems in the Highlands are, at this day, replete with similar expressions applied to any land viewed over a part of the sea.

That *the top of the waves* is a faithful translation, is afferted with a positive tone: But the arguments advanced, with a view to derive the name of our island from it, are only the children of imagination; and, therefore, left to be crushed or cherished at the mercy of the reader. No attempt, however, hath been made to mislead him, as the Translator does not pretend to support his opinion, either by the testimony of history, or the voice of tradition. It is, notwithstanding, countenanced by the universal custom of the Celtic nations, of never bestowing a name on any object that was not highly significant and characteristic.

This

forth the hand of friendship to receive us. Welcome, said he, are the sons of ocean, when they come in peace. Our deers are many: Our shells are full. The tales of our bards are pleasant; and why should the stranger mourn in our hall?

The feast was spread with mirth, and we blessed the foes of our fathers.

Minvas * shone in the hall of her father, like the first beam of the rising sun, when it smiles on the dewy plains. Many chiefs sought the love of the maid; but she turned her eyes from the mighty, and fixed them on Moralt.

Nor hills, nor warriors were mine. I went to the battle alone. The foes of Lochlin had fallen by my hand; but my fame was not heard.

Go, said the maid; fight the battles of other kings. Gather thy fame in a distant land;

send

This is the only evidence we can reasonably expect, in support of the origin of terms which have made their way to us, from a people destitute of the use of letters, and consequently of any other means of conveyance, than the signification of words.

* Min-bhas, *soft palm.*

send it before thee to Minvas, and she will own thy love.

I went to Erin's * king. Many of his foes fell by my sword. My name was heard in song,

* All the places which lay to the west, were antiently denominated *Era*; as Erin, Ireland; Er-gael, Argyle, signifying the western Celtæ, in opposition to those who inhabited the eastern coast of Scotland.

The Rev. Mr Whitaker gives a very different account of the matter; and claims no small portion of merit from the discoveries he has made, and the victories he has gained over all the critics and historians who have written on this subject. If these claims are properly founded, no apology will be due to the reader for laying them before him.

' Ar-gathel, Iar-gael, or Ar-gyle. This name has puzzled all the critics and historians. But it is nothing more than the IRISH. The Britons being universally called *Gathel*, and *Gael*, such of them as went over into Ire-land, Iar-in, or Er-in, must naturally have received the appellation of Iar-gael, Er-gael, Ar-gael, or the Ir-ish Britons; and the appellation remains, to this day, among the Irish, in their customary appellation for their own language, Caelich Eir-inach, or the Ir-ish British.' *Whitaker's Genuine History of the Britons*, p. 287.

Ostentation never raised her giddy head with less reason than in the above extract. It is astonishing how a writer

song, and my fame travelled over many seas. The daughters of Innis-fail spread their white arms

of Mr Whitaker's penetration could attempt to gather laurels in the field of Celtic etymology. Ignorant of every dialect of that language, he deceives himself by the similarity of sound, or by pronouncing letters, which, according to the genius of the language, ought to be quiescent. Laying, thus, the basis of his hypothesis on a false foundation, he proceeds to erect a structure, which even the beautiful manner of his execution cannot rescue from censure; and, he almost compells his intelligent readers to forget that respect which is due to him, as a gentleman of genius and learning.

The name of *Argyle* has never puzzled any critic or historian who understood the language of its inhabitants, as there are not two words in it easier defined than those that compose it, *i. e.* Era, *west*; and Gael, the general name of the Celtic nations.

The Britons are here said to be universally termed Gathel and Gael.—As much knowledge in the Galic as generally falls to the share of a school-boy, would be sufficient to inform Mr Whitaker, that the names are both the same; that the *th* in the middle or end of words, after a broad vowel, are universally silent; and, although written by some antient authors, are never pronounced. A thorough knowledge of the fundamental rules of Celtic grammar would have saved Mr Whitaker and his readers

arms before me in vain. When peace smiled on the land, I returned to the maid of snow.

The an immense deal of trouble, and rescued the subject from that obscurity into which his ignorance of them has thrown it, by creating several names out of one. The whole argument is founded on a supposition, that the term *Gael* was applicable to no other people than the Britons.

The word *Gael* signifies literally *Whites*, and is the name by which we find the principal inhabitants of Europe, towards the west, first distinguished in antient history. Accordingly, all the remains of that people, to this day, call themselves *Gael*; as Gaelic-albinach, the language of the Gaels in Albin; Gaelic Erinach, the language of the Gaels in Ireland, and Gaelic-ualsh the language of the Gaels in Wales.

The inhabitants of Britain were never called *Gael* from their country, but from their language. The appellation, therefore, always was, and is, at this day, applied promiscuously to the inhabitants of both islands, who continued to speak the antient Celtic.

That the Irish call their own language ' Gaelic-erinach,' is an undisputed truth. But the subsequent definition of it, or ' *the Irish British*,' furnishes a glaring instance of the boldness with which this author advances the chimera of his own brain in the face of well attested facts. Does not Mr Whitaker know, that the Galicians in Spain spoke this language? Does he not know that the Gauls in France spoke it? Does not he know that the Irish themselves

The sun lay asleep, and the moon wandered from cloud to cloud, when the hall of Dunairm appeared. From the skirts of a birchen grove the breath of night conveyed to my ears a sound soft as the breath of summer.—' Go; and, if thou fall, Minvas will bathe thy sweet memory with her tears.'

My soul, that never trembled before, shook with dread and horror. I saw Minvas; and stately was the warrior who stood by her side.

I bent

selves spoke it? Why then pretend to confine it to the Britons?

Ignorance of the Celtic language, which may, in some cases, be held forth as a shield for Mr Whitaker, will not here avail him. A writer far less versant in the voluminous history of antiquity, must have known, that, when Argyle received its name, Gael, or Celtæ, was applied to many nations of Europe. What apology, therefore, shall candour find for an author who could thus flatter his own vanity, and gratify the prejudice of his countrymen, at the expence of truth, and violation of these sacred principles of honour, on which every historian ought to value himself?—But he is not singular in his conduct. The utmost efforts of the mind seem to extend no further than to *propose* well. The *execution* generally compels us to regret each others weakness, and lament that human nature, even in her noblest appearance, is clogged with infirmities.

I bent my bow.—Go, said I to an arrow, pierce that breast of falshood. Let no other warrior search for fame to please that heart of pride.

The steel entered her white bosom *. Her variegated garment is spread on the heath. Her long hair is bathed in her blood. Her groans are mingled with the sighs of night.

Whence came the meteor of death, cried the warrior?—From an arm of strength, I replied; and raised my spear.

Son of gloomy night, said the astonished youth, thy arm is strong because the foe was feeble. The spear of the mighty never rose before a dark heart like thine. But thy surly ghost

---

* This passage furnishes an instance of northern barbarity, of which nothing similar is found among the Caledonians. Little credit, however, would be due to the assertions of the bard, had he brought this warrior into the poem under a contemptible character, as he was descended of the hereditary foes of the Caledonians. But the appearance which he makes throughout the piece, leaves no room to suspect that the poet was led by any such disgraceful partiality. The present is, perhaps, the only crime he could commit, for which his subsequent conduct would not entitle him to the reader's forgiveness,

ghost shall forthwith depart from its dwelling, and mingle with the sons of the wind, where thy boneless arm shall never raise the steel against the lovely.

Long we fought on the heath. The groans of Minvas were lost in the clash of our steel. The spear of my foe at last gave way, and he fell before me. The moon looked forth from the skirts of a dark cloud, and I beheld my friend, the brother of Minvas, in his blood.

And art thou fallen, my brother, said the faultering voice of the maid; and shall thy father never behold thy return from the chace?—Oh, Moralt! on what distant land does thy spear rise against the mighty?—No brother of mine shall now call thee from the fields of thy fame. But thou wilt some time return, my hero, and raise the tomb of Minvas near the groves of our former loves.——

I drew the steel from the breast of the lovely. My tears mingled with the red stream from her bosom. She opened her faint eyes, and beheld her Moralt's hands bathed in her blood.—She shrieked herself into a ghost. I strove to grasp it in my arms; but it fled with
horror

horror from my embrace, and rose on a beam of the moon.

Four stones mark the dwelling of the hero: Near it rose the tomb of the lovely. The virgins often give the tear of pity as they pass: The tenants of the bush sing their songs of woe. All night I sit, and listen to the wind. Dark clouds frown on me as they roll over my head. The children of the air shun me with horror.

The chief of Dunairm mourns lonely in his hall. Many tears he sheds for the fallen. By times he feels his childrens tomb. The passing blast bears on its wings his voice of woe to distant lands. He lifts his spear no more:—But I lift his spear. I lift it against my father's house. The son of Dunairm fell by my hand; but the foes which ought to fall by him, shall also come down. Minvas fell before the moon. Before the moon shall I meet her father's foes. I will meet them, O king; but I will not return. I will depart like the angry storm which has long poured its frosty venom on the plains. The fairest lily of the field perished before it: The vegetable race sink by its wrath.

wrath. The fallen ftag lies at the bottom of the rock. The children of the wing are mute. The leafy garment has fled from the blafted oak: The foreft fhakes its fcattered locks in the angry face of heaven. The peafant fhuns its wrath near the gleam of his oaks. But the father of kindnefs looks forth at noon on the mourning plains with pity. He difplays the bright locks of his awful beauty. The foe of nature flies from his ftrength. The hills fhake the fnow from their heathy locks, and fmile at his departure.

Sit thou on the heath till morning, leader of chiefs, and I fhall fall alone in the midft of thy foes; left it be faid, 'The foe of the lovely is among us, we fhall not profper.'

Mournful is thy tale, Moralt, faid the king; but thou muft not fall alone.—Albin's fons will never fleep on the heath, while ftrangers fight her battles. Thou art a beam of fire in the day of danger; but raife not, Moralt, the fteel againft thy friends. The mighty muft fall at laft. The frowns of winter purfue the footfteps of the fmiling fummer.—Minvas was a fun-beam in the feafon of her lovelinefs.

Few

Few could meet the son of Dunairm in the days of his wrath. Not unmarked are their dwelling among the tenants of the grave; nor unheard their fame in the breath of song. But the spear of thy fathers, Moralt, mourns in thy hand. The generous steel is ashamed to reek with the blood of Lochlin.

It is the spear of Dunairm's chief, said Moralt, that reeks with the blood of his foes:— Mine shall never more rise in battle. It lies buried * in the tomb of the lovely, beneath the tree of the rustling leaf. Strong was the arm which ought to wield this spear; but he defends Minvas from the frowns of fury ghosts in the land of clouds †. And shall the foe

triumph

* It was a custom among the antient Celtæ, to bury or destroy every weapon which had been used in the commission of any crime or unlucky accident; as it was imagined, that the ghosts of the injured were endowed with power to render every effort of such weapons fruitless in all succeeding contests. We do not, however, hear of any desire of revenge being entertained by the ghosts of those who had been killed in fair combat; for such did not consider themselves as injured.

† Some have been led to conclude, from this passage, that the antients were of opinion, that the ghosts of the

departed

triumph over his father in the days of his feeble years?—No, O King! they shall never insult his gray hairs while I can wield this spear.

Long mayest thou wield it in renown, O hero! said Canard; but hearken to the woes of others. I too might mourn the fall of the lovely; but sighs call not forth the tenants of the tomb.

Graceful on the hills was Culalin*, the maid of the hand of snow. Her dark hair rose on the

---

departed remained in a state of hostility with each other. —The words, I believe, will admit of another explanation. The idea of the young warrior's falling in defence of his sister, ran so strong in the mind of Moralt, that a disordered imagination might represent him as still employed in that office after death; and that the bard has, perhaps, given the real words of the distracted hero, and not the received opinion of the antients, who seem to have entertained a milder notion of a future state, than to make it a theatre for a repetition of crimes, or a scene for the decision of future contests. This opinion would be clogged with one material difficulty. What would become of the remains of those ghosts who might fall in these imaginary wars?

* Cul-alin, of *cul*, a poetical name for a lady's fine locks: and *alin*, graceful —The name of Alan, or Allen, in Scotland and Ireland, is from the same root.

the wind like the raven's wing. The heaving of her white breast was as the downy bosom of the swan, when the soft waves meet it in gladness. The beauty of each virgin vanished when the daughter of Sonner appeared. Graceful was the mother of my sons, and gladness shone in my hall when her soft voice joined the harp.

Guigan, the daughter of Ainer, had tasted my secret embrace before I saw Culalin, and she turned the red eye of envy on the pride of women. She came to Culalin in the season of her solitude, and spoke the words of deceit.

Pleasant are the smiles of the mid-day sun, Culalin! cool the shade beneath the birchen boughs. The hunters are distant far. The sea has borne her waves to other lands, and left our rocks to raise their dark heads before the kindly breeze. Come, daughter of Sonner, and taste the sweets of noon.

They wandered through the forest. A tall rock within the verge of ocean's bed, affords a grateful shade. Sleep shut the eyes of Culalin. Guigan plet her long hair with thongs, and fixed them to the cliffy rock. Her hands of snow are bound: Her feet are tied to a stone. The maid of the gloomy soul saw the coming of the flood. She rejoiced in the blackness of her deeds, and fled.

Ocean came with all his tumbling waves. Culalin startled at the sound.—Where art thou, my friend? Save me, Guigan, from the hostile flood.—

The rocks answered in pity to her groans: Sighs issued from each hollow cave. But soon shall ye cease to mourn for my love, ye sons of the rock! Another wave, and she lies peaceful beneath the stream. The retiring flood shall leave her as food for the ravenous children of the sea.

The strength of thy brother's arm, Guigan, though he was my best, my dearest friend, was no shield to thee. Alas! the hero fell before my sword. He who had saved my life in battle, died by my hand. Thou also sleepest near him, cruel maid, and thy ghost often frowns on me in the season of dreams.'

But thou, Culalin, of the raven locks! pleasant art thou in thy loveliness, as thou smilest on the couch of my slumbers. No surly looks

are

are thine. No traveller shuns thy dwelling *
in the season of the moon. Often doest thou
raise thy shrill voice on thy rocks, and warn the
mariner of the coming storm †. He hears the
unerring sound, and retires within the peace-
ful bosom of the creek. In safety he views
the

* It was only the ghosts of those who had been guilty
of some crime in their lifetime, that were supposed to wan-
der and attack the nightly traveller. The punishment of
such crimes was thought to consist in wandering near their
graves, till they met with one whom they sought, and
compelled to make restitution to the persons or their de-
scendants, whom they had injured in their lifetime; after
which, it was thought they were permitted to sleep in
peace.—This notion, if not more rational, was at least
more agreeable to the minds of men, than those of a purer
religion.

† Storms frequently rage with great fury at sea, while
it is perfectly calm on the land, before the arrival of the
winds which occasion them. These violent agitations in
the ocean, cause the waves to roar with such fury on the
rocks, that they are heard at the distance of several miles.
Experience has taught the inhabitants on the coast to know,
by this noise, that the storm is coming, some time before
it arrives. The antients were of opinion, that this was
occasioned by the ghosts of those who had been drowned,
who were considered as monitors to warn men of ap-
proaching danger.

the conflict of the waves, and blesses the friendly sound of thy rocks, thou watcher of the nightly storms!

Thus have I slain my friend, Moralt; yet my spear rises with success against the foe.—The lovely rise but to fall: The mighty gather strength but to sink.

Canard said, and his mournful words ceased.—Silent and gloomy sat the listening host. Sighs broke forth at the close of the tale of woe. The forest ceased to wave its dark head: The short-limbed heath stood still. Clouds were fixed in the face of heaven. No rocks contended with the blast. Peace was proclaimed among the vegetable race; for the wind ceased to travel *.

What

---

* This is supposed to be the situation of surrounding objects, while the two foregoing episodes were relating, though not described till now.

Callum Ruadh, a bard still alive in the Highlands, has given a similar description of the attention paid to antient bards during the rehearsal of their pieces. I have endeavoured to attone, as far as I could, for the injury it has suffered in the translation, by throwing the passage into rhyme.

When

What faint beam, with its half formed smile, gladens the cheek of the east? The moon is asleep in her heathy bed, and the sun is not yet

When battles ceas'd, and warriors sheath'd the sword,
Bards join'd the circle round the burning ourd.
The deeds of heroes then employ'd the song:
Attentive were the old, and mute the young.
The sons of discord ceas'd to search for blood;
And life-inspiring casks half empty stood.
Then Beauty's daughters got no half-stol'n glance,
And maids in rich attire forgot the dance.
The sons of mirth neglected to form the ring,
And the bow ceas'd to cross the trembling string.
The finny tribe stood list'ning in the flood,
And silence sway'd her sceptre o'er the wood.
The foe of deers lean'd on the fire of death,
And the roe-buck in safety cropt the heath.
The welcome theme brought forth the pleasing dew,
When every chief receiv'd what praise was due.
Woe had not then engaged each melting tear;
For pleasing admiration got her share.
The love of valour fir'd each warrior's breast:
Proud of his chieftain's feats, he rear'd his crest.
The fires reflected on their former days;
The sons were eager to deserve such praise.
Joy sparkled in the face which age made pale;
Each bless'd the mouth that told the welcome tale.

yet prepared to ſtep forth in the brightneſs of his beauty.———It is Minvas, the maid of the ſnowy boſom, coming with her hundred meteors to light Moralt, the hero of other lands, the bearer of her father's ſhield, to the fields of death.

In wrath the virgin comes not to her friends. She purſues the gloom of night from our mountains. The morning-ſtar trembles in her hand. She comes like the firſt beam which the ſun ſends forth to proclaim his approach before he leaves his bed of reſt in the eaſt.

Why doſt thou fly from us in haſte, maid of the mild aſpect?—But thou haſt left morning on our hills; and thy dim form has diſappeared, like a cloud of miſt on the lake, which vaniſhes before the face of the fire of brightneſs.

MORDUTH,

MORDUTH,

BOOK III.

FAINT beams smiled in the east. Gloomy night fled on her wings of speed. The twinkling stars retired to other lands; and the sun prepared to raise his fair head, when a bard appeared on the heath with his song of pride.

Swanar, the chief of an hundred chiefs: He that is strong as a rock in the sea, as a hill on the land, sends his terrible song to the sons of the mountains.

His eagles are on their wings. His hawks, the followers of his spear, are round him. His ravens have winged their journey round his ships, over many seas. The devouring tribes ask for food. Does the chief of this land grant them his warriors for their feast; or, does he bend before the mighty, and offer them

them his deer?—Speak, ye who fly in battle; for many deaths are in the points of Lochlin's spears.

The words of Swanar are great, bard of the hoary locks! His words are great, because his foes are few. But, sit thou here, and taste the shell of friendship, son of songs; and, when thou returnest to Lochlin's king, tell him that the ravenous sons of the wing have but followed their food over many seas*. Bid him advance with his thousands. Tell him that our arms are strong, and that our souls are bright.

The bard heard the words of the king, and departed in the pride of his haughty steps. He talked of ghosts as he went, because he foresaw the fall of many.

As the angry storm from the north gathers all its winds, and rains, and clouds, when it prepares

---

* When any bird of prey was seen sitting on the mast of a ship, it was considered as a very bad omen. It was imagined they were endowed with the gift of foreknowledge, by which they followed ships for some time before they were wrecked. The Highlanders, to this day, consider any vessel on which they are seen, as doomed to destruction.

prepares to rush along the plains and pour its fury on the mountains; so gathered Swanar the warriors of his land. Their shields were like the dark clouds of night: Their faces like the stars looking forth by times from their sable skirts.

The force of Albin advanced like a ridge of mighty waves, whose strength is increased by the hostile breath of many blasts. Above is the course of the storm. The broad-faced moon looks down by times. The mariner hears the hideous sound with horror. He trusts in the strength of his bark, and prepares to meet the danger which he cannot shun.

O hunter of Corri! how shall I describe the deeds of our arms?—Thou hast seen Morcraig. It rears its head aloft, and drags the clouds from heaven to clothe its shaggy brows. A mighty torrent tumbles from its top. Its downward journey is an hundred times the length of the tallest warrior that ever raised the massy shield.—Thou hast seen the contest between the flood and the rocks below;—but thou never didst,—hunter of Corri! thou never shall see strife like ours.

As the feeble twig bends before the storm, when angry ghosts contend in the sky; so bent the race of Lochlin before the king of Albin. Swanar saw his coming, and thrice he shook his spear.

But thou shakest it in vain, son of the sea. Albin's chief is a rock which laughs at the storm. The strongest waves shrink with terror from its angry brows.

But I never shrunk with terror, said the king of the north. My arm is strong as an hundred storms. Rocks, woods, and mountains, oppose not me. Have not I defeated the force of the ocean?—Stormy seas spread themselves round my coasts, and cry with all their threatening waves, 'Thou shalt go no further.' But ye cry in vain, ye haughty seas! Have not I defeated your strength; and shall the king of this land stand before me?

Such were the words of the two chiefs; but, when they raised their terrible spears, the earth shook around, trees fell torn from their roots. Rocks groaned beneath their feet, and,

and, forsaking their beds of rest, rolled away with terror.

Many swords rose around: Many arrows fled from the yew. Many warriors stood at a distance, and viewed the strife of the two kings. But the shield of Swanar sank, and his people trembled. The spear of Morduth rose to end the strife; but the thoughts of the valiant darted on his soul, and he spared the shieldless breast.

Moralt was forward in the bloody contest. A ghost ascends from each stroke of the hero. Distant stood a chief of Lochlin, tall as a tree by the stream. The sons of Albin fall back from his shield, as the waves from a rock.

So stands the oak of many years. The course of the storm is abroad; but thy head, daughter of strength and beauty, is exalted, and thou regardest not the wrath of the blast. Safety is behind thee; and the hunter shuns the storm near thy stately trunk. Thou art his shield from the violence of its rage.—So stood the feeble behind the shield of the chief *.

K   Moralt

* To do justice to the merits of an opponent, appears to be

Moralt raised his spear against the mighty son of the sea. The meeting of the two heroes was terrible. Rocks answered to the groans of their steel. The torn heath fled from the struggling of their footsteps: Trees fell before the strife of their spears. The sons of little men saw it, and were afraid.

Long the heroes fought, and long the admiring hosts beheld the gleam of their steel. But both sank together on the heath, and the bloody stream was from both their sides, when Moralt spoke:

I am low, warrior!—my spear shall no more meet the shield of the mighty: My sword shall no more glitter in the strife of heroes.—I have yet one brother, Solva of the massy shield. He pursues the deer on the banks of Bawnar.—If thou wisheft to fall by the mighty, meet him, and thy fame will be great in song.—

And

be one of the highest triumphs which human nature can boast of obtaining over that narrowness of mind, which the cultivation of modern politeness seems but to cherish. Nature, however rears her head with dignity, and claims several honours of this kind due to her children. But these most frequently occur among a people whom the haughtiness of science has termed *Barbarians.*

And have I raised the steel against thee, O Moralt!—Hath my hand laid the son of my father low?—Thou who taught me to wield the spear!—But never more will I wield it.—Reach me thy hand of friendship;—I will grasp it to my bosom. We will travel together to the dwellings of our fathers.—One cloud will be our bed in the land of ghosts.

The mournful host heard the words of Solva. The race of Lochlin fled to their dark ships.—Morduth dropt a tear over the heroes, and bade the battle cease.—The huge stone rose above the mighty. Near it is the rustling of an aged oak The whirlwind stops betimes on its boughs.: The meteors of night dance round it.—The traveller shuns it in the season of stars: With horror he shuns the unfrequented path. —Two ghosts are its guard; and nought but the roaring storm is permitted to visit the tombs of the heroes *

* This is all that the Translator could collect of the admired and well known poem of Morduth. Several old persons remember to have heard other episodes, which are now lost. Where these were introduced, cannot now be ascertained. In the places where it is here divided into books, it is customary for the Bards, or others who rehearse it, to pause, take snuff, and make remarks.

CHIEF OF SCARLAW.

LONG have I followed the footsteps of the stag on the hills of Fuarven. Often has the summer sun returned from his southern journey; and, with the animating strength of his kindly beams, called forth the flowery offspring of the vale. These, for a while, have waved their golden locks, and smiled upon their nodding stalks: But they vanished before the breath of the north; and their children have afterwards sprung up, and filled their places.

Chiefs of old! ye have also fallen: But your children have not filled your places *. Many years have been mine. I behold no companions

---

* Complaints of this nature have been pronounced with great severity in all ages, against the rising generation. As age

companions of my youth, but the rocks and the woods. Five chiefs have arisen in my days, and

age and infirmities enfeeble and contract the powers of the body, they are generally productive of similar effects upon the mind. Old men are liable to be biassed by groundless prejudices and ungenerous sentiments. They affect to despise the world, because they can no longer enjoy it; and are apt, upon that account, to display their ill nature and chagrin on every thing around them. They seldom fail to draw partial comparisons between the companions of their juvenile years, and the youths that surround them in their decline of life.

Thus Ossian represents those that immediately followed the Fingalian race, as *little men.* Morguth, who succeeded Ossian, tells us, that, in the days of his gray hairs, the feeble tried in vain to raise the spears of their mighty fathers; and the same strain has been sung by almost every bard to our own days.

These poems were handed down with great care to succeeding ages, who did not presume to call in question the veracity of what was advanced by their favourite bards, but understood every word in a literal sense.

The human mind, eager of prying into the obscurity of former ages, and always creating difficulties it cannot surmount, began to form gigantic notions of the heroes of these poems. All the bards agreed, that mankind was degenerating, with great rapidity, from the strength and stature

and funk into the grave in the winter of life. They held the shield against the foe, and spread the feast before the stranger. The ghosts of their enemies fled from their swords in the day of battle.—The heroes lie in Killeusan: Their fame is in the song of bards.

Little Gruiman of the surly brow came afterwards. He fled in the time of danger; and sunk beneath the arm of a feeble foe. He was laid under the stone, with the dry burial of the little soul.—No virgin of disordered locks was seen near his tomb *.

Sons

stature of the antients. The imagination at last, shaking off the fetters of reason, and overleaping the bounds of probability, looked back, at full liberty, on the stature of their ancestors, and magnified every generation successively, till it presented the mind with the idea of that monster called *a Giant*.

The bards cherished these notions, which the vulgar swallowed with a voracious appetite, and satiated their hearers with a *quantum sufficit* of the marvellous, as they could now magnify the strength, stature, and actions of their heroes *ad infinitum*. But these magazines of bombast were of short duration, as the best bards of all ages have always expressed a hearty contempt for this species of composition.

* It is with pleasure we read such passages in antient poetry, as represent the ladies the patrons of virtue.

Sons of the few years, ye that be but of yesterday! the strength that was mine is yours. Lend me the arm of your youth.—Carry me to the towering top of Benmore, that I may view the hills that wave their heath-brown locks round the strath of Fingal *, the warrior of other days.

O

It has been remarked of great poets, That they are very sparing of general encomiums on the fair-sex; and the present compliment seems to come undesignedly. Their contemptuous neglect of a pusillanimous chief, is here mentioned, with a view to darken his character, not to illuminate theirs. But the eye of penetration may look a little further, and view them in their genuine colours, punishing vice with their frowns, and rewarding virtue with their smiles.

Encouraged by the silence of some antient poets, certain modern ones have presumed to pronounce general censures upon the sex. But, had these gentlemen given us their compositions with as little reserve as the present bard seems to have done, and presented the image of their own breast with equal ingenuity, there is great reason to think, that several passages similar to this, would appear against them in their writings. No poet of reputation, however, has ventured to deviate from nature, so far as to make the soft eye of beauty smile on a despicable character among the males.

* Fingal, *the Celtic hero.* The word *Gael*, (the Celtæ of

the

O Ossian, king of songs! thou who drew the tear from the eye: Thou who brought the

the Roman authors), signifies literally *Whites*, and was probably once the universal appellation of all the Europeans, in opposition to the *Blacks* of the warmer climates. All the remnants of that once great people, call themselves *Gael*, in whatever country they are scattered. The word *White*, and their own name *Gael*, are both written and pronounced the same at this day.

The Rev. Mr Whitaker has placed his opinion on this subject, in direct opposition to all the Celtæ themselves; and asserts, that it is 'a designation too effeminate for the bold and ferocious Celtæ.' Whatever effeminate notion that gentleman may have formed of the *white* part of mankind, it is most certain, that all the Celtæ had the misfortune to be of that colour; and, therefore, truth compelled them to adopt the name of *Whites*, whatever unfavourable opinions antiquaries may form of their valour from it. If the reader has any desire to see etymology in the most abject state of dejection to which pride and rashness ever reduced her, he may consult Mr Whitaker's definition of the word *Gael*, page 122. The passage is too long for insertion, and, may I be permitted to add, too feeble for opposition. After producing the names of several tribes among the antient Britons, he tell us, that they all signified *Woodlanders*: That *Coil* is the same with *Gathel*, which, he says signifies a wood among the Highlanders and Irish at present.—The assertion, however, is

not

the foe to the ground!—Royal mourner of Selma's race! where shall I search for thy tomb? The sons of negligence have suffered the waving heath to cover it.—The hearer of tales round the burning ourd meets thy words; and he melts before them.—The course of the storm is abroad; but thy tomb it meets not. The voice of its rage is loud amongst the projecting cliffs: But thy narrow dwelling, O king of bards! it passes over in silence. No huge stone rears its lofty head there, to compel the flying winds to stop their rapid journey, and, with murmuring accents, salute the mighty that lie below.—But roll on, voice of the north! The fame of Ossian regards thee not:—Thyself art but for a season. Tho' the feeble branches of the wood bend before thee, and the waving heath kneels at thy approach, when thou art gone, they erect their heads, and forget thy strength.—But the strength of

Ossian's

not true; and every subsequent argument deduced from it, is totally destitute of support. There are not two words in the antient language of Britain, more different in the orthography, sound, and signification, than *Coil*, a wood; and *Gathel*, the same as Gael, the universal name of the Celtic nations.

Ossian's song shall never be forgot, while the oaks of Albin blaze before the tenants of her glens.

Thy head, Gruimore, contends not with little hills. Lofty mountains rise by thy side; but they sink before thee. The hunter on the top points to the stormy dwelling of the king of the ocean *, whose wing of strength fought the battles of Albin, when her sons were weak. The clouds of heaven salute thee as they pass: The dreams of thy sons are many in the season of sleep. The music of thy woods proclaims the welcome of the rising sun, ere he leaves his watery bed in the eastern ocean. The stag starts at the sound; and his mate is absent. He pants for the safety of her he beholds not. —Stare not so wildly, son of the branchy forehead. The partner of thy joy crops the flowery food in yon hollow glen, along the border of the silver stream: The wanton steps of her lovely fawn are round her.

Ye hills of the heathy locks, on whose slopping sides I have passed the days of my youth, when my steps were swift in the chace: Let me

---

* The whale poetically called so.—This refers to an episode in a great work, most of which is in the Translator's hands, but is excluded from the present volume, on account of its length.

me behold you once more, while my words are heard, before the child of my grandson say, ' The breath of the bard is fled.'--Where is the music that is sweeter than that of thy winged inhabitants? Where is the wind that is fleeter than thy stags?—Often have I pursued the sons of swiftness: But the feeble who fell behind, and she who staid to protect her young, never fell by my hand. Be kind then to me, ye children of youth; for I, fall behind in the chace. No steps of speed are mine: My trembling joints shake as I move. I fill no more the footsteps of the hound!

O ye, who have seen the battles of my youth! when the dead were behind, and the flying foes of Albin before me, shake your heads in pity to the weakness of my arm!—But ye behold it not, warriors of other days! ye are in the land of ghosts. Ye retire to the tomb when the watchful cock proclaims the approach of day *.

Sons

---

* This opinion is not confined to the antient's alone. The Highlanders, at this day, inform us, with great solemnity, that the ghosts of the deceased wander from sun-
set

Sons of little deeds, ye who have never been in the strife of heroes, hearken to a tale of former years; and learn to unsheath the sword when the ships of Lochlin appear.

The Chief of Scarlaw pursued his deer far distant from Gruimore, on the hills of Ardcraig, near the tumbling of the waves. His sons, who followed him in the chace, were ten. The oaks lay ready for the flint; and the panting of the hounds was round the falling stag, when Dalav spoke.—

A set till the cock crows; but the most dangerous time of encountering them is about mid-night. These nightly champions, however, were of great service to mankind in several respects; for, it was confidently asserted, that the ghost would be revenged on any person who had defrauded him or his posterity of their property.

These ghosts were once a strong bar against injustice; but, as the commission of crimes became more frequent, new schemes were invented to screen the guilty After the introduction of Christianity, it was suggested to the populace, that, if they would draw a circle round them on the appearance of a ghost, in name of the Trinity, &c. the ghost durst never enter that line of circumvallation. Accordingly, this method of carrying on war against the pious inhabitants of the air, is now practised with great success.

A sail raises her head above the restless waves of ocean. The wrath of the storm is fierce, but she regards it not. Daughter of beauty, strength, and speed! come to the woods of Scarlaw. The warriors of thy dark bosom shall taste the joys of our hall, and carry our fame to a distant land, where the friends of Albin will be many.—Ashian! strike not yet the flint: Delay the feast until the strangers arrive.

Nor feast shall they taste, nor fame carry, said the chief. Let every son of mine grasp his shield. I see death on our coast; but he shall taste the blood of strangers.—My sons may fall; but their fame shall survive them.

Chief of the open door *, said Dalav, such were not wont to be thy words, when the stranger came to Scarlaw's hall. Often have

the

---

* This refers to a species of hospitality observed at this day, by the common people, in the Highlands. If the severity of the weather compels them to shut their doors, they are sure to set them open when they sit down to meat, lest a traveller, by seeing the door shut, might be induced to pass by, and thereby deprive them of the pleasure which they always enjoy in entertaining a stranger. A man who sits down to feast with his door shut, is considered as a disgrace to the clan to whom he belongs.

the fingers of difpatch fpread the feaft at his approach *. His feat was next thee, near the flame of the oaks; and the joy of thy foul was great, when he fpoke the tales of other lands. Why then befpeak death to meet the fons of the waves?

Son of my youth, faid the chief, thefe are Lochlin's fons, who never feaft in the hall of ftrangers. Their joy is in the fall of Albin's race.

Then no joy fhall be theirs, replied the youth of the rifing foul. The fword of Albin is not wielded by a feeble arm.—Shall I go, and inquire their numbers, that warriors may prepare to meet them †?

Yes,

---

* When a traveller was feen coming towards a houfe, victuals were provided for him by the time he arrived. The large ranges of mountains which fometimes feparate the inhabited valleys from each other, rendered fuch a piece of expedition very often neceffary. But, when the gueft came abruptly, he was under a neceffity of putting up with what was at hand. Hence came the well known invitation of *taking bread and cheefe till better meat was ready*.

† The Caledomans always confidered it difgraceful to meet their enemies with a fuperior number, till the conduct of their invaders taught them the contrary.

Yes, my son, thou shalt go; but let thy people be near thee, lest many spears rise against one, and the joy of thy father cease.

* Scalan, the son of Shearhuil, opened his mouth; and the words of the little soul came forth.

If in haste we get behind the rocks of Scritan, we may sink the spear of death in the breast of every warrior, as he climbs the cliffs. Then Lochlin's race shall fall; and no danger be near the sons of Albin.

Lover of days, said the chief, the mighty fight not thus their battles. We seek not for safety, but for Albin's foes; and we will meet them when their arm is strongest. Let us go to the hall of arms, and call forth every warrior with his sword of battle, that the sons of Albin may be strong behind the shields of their fathers.

I was then with Benguth, Scarlaw's bard. The fame of his song brought me from Gruimore. My joy was great when I heard the sound of arms.

Son

---

* Scalan, *shadow.* Shear-huil, *squint-eyed.*

Son of the song, said Scarlaw's chief, Lochlin's race is near. One ship is seen, and she is not alone. Go to the banks of Dluchoil: Meet them; and speak the words of Albin when her foes approach †.

Benguth

† These, in general, contained an inquiry, whether they came as friends or foes. This practice came almost to our own days. The unfortunate M'Donald of Glenco, put the same question to the commander of the party sent by King William to massacre an innocent people. The officer answered, that they came as friends. Accordingly they were treated with all the demonstrations of kindness and civility which assiduity could suggest, or hospitality bestow, for several days. But this party afterwards, in the dead of night, pierced with their daggers, those hearts, on whose generosity they had feasted so long; and murdered the chief, with seventy of his people; without giving them the smallest opportunity of drawing a weapon in their own defence.

When the Highlanders were a little recovered from the consternation into which this piece of treachery had thrown them, the bards poured forth their tears in elegies for their murdered friends. But they appear to have lost part of their former elegance on this occasion. The subject was entirely new. Their antient poetry contained nothing similar to it; and their language could furnish them with no epithets capable to express the baseness of the assassins.

Benguth went to meet the foe :—He went, and the locks of age were his shield.

Sons of the distant land, ye are welcome to Albin's coast.—Come ye to empty the shell at the feast of friendship, to rejoice with the race of Albin round the burning oaks, to taste the joys of the hall of warriors, and pursue the footsteps of the stag with the sons of the chace?—Or does the forward point of the spear raise the arms of the mighty against you? Speak, warriors; the swords of Albin are many.—

And let them be strong too, said a chief of Lochlin, what then?—Thy words, son of age, terrify not us. We have met the breath of the storm, when it was louder than thine; yet were we not afraid. Go to Scarlaw's gray-haired chief. Tell him, that his ghost must attend this night at the tomb of Lochlin's king, whom he slew in his youth. Bid him come forth with his shield of strength. Tell him,

But the period is too recent, and the characters alluded to, too well known, to admit of a translation of these poems, without giving offence to individuals, and recalling events, which it is the business of humanity to bury in oblivion.

him, that the swords which await him are not in the hands of the feeble.

Benguth stroaked his beard.—He shook his hoary head; and returned to the hall of Scarlaw.

Come they to mourn at the tombs of their fathers; or, does their forward spear call us to battle?

To mourn they come not, O chief! Their words are big with the death of many.—

Then of themselves be that many, Benguth.—The sons of Albin will meet them, as the rock meets the breath of the eastern storm, when the furious waves tumble in disorder behind it.

Flaian, youngest son of mine, be thou near the shield of thy father, lest the sword of strength oppose thee, and thou fall before the weight of thy arm be known.—Dalav, son of my youth, I appoint no place for thee. Pursue danger: Thy arm can meet it. If a shield of Albin sink, search for him who brought it down. His fall will raise thy fame. Let the safety of my people be thy care.—Raspan, Ogier, and Bawn, ye are young, my sons:

Few

few battles have rolled before you. Be near me, and obſerve my ſword by times; for I have fought beſide the warriors of former days.

We moved behind the ſteps of the chief.—Lochlin's army approached: We met on Rovan heath. Scarlaw ſtruck his echoing ſhield. Rattling ſpears roſe around. Lochlin's ſons ſuſtained the ſhock.—Shield met ſword, and ſword met ſhield: The voice of the ſteel returned from the diſtant rocks. The deeds of the mighty pointed out the chief to Lochlin's race: Shields of ſtrength met his ſpear. His ſteps were forward in the battle: But on either ſide Albin's ſons fell back; for the chief was ſurrounded by the arms of youth.

Dalav ſaw the marks of his father's forward ſpear. I fought near the youth. I heard the ſecret groans of his ſoul, as he mourned his ſlow ſteps in battle. Son of Gruimore, ſaid he, the chief is alone: His foes are many; and no arm of ſtrength is near. Go, be thou the ſhield of his back, leſt the coward ſpear come behind, and the fame of Albin ceaſe.

I went

I went to aid the chief; but who can speak the strength of his arm! The meteors of death were in the gleam of his steel. Foes sank before him: Ghosts rose behind. His steps were in the midst of bloody streams: The heath of Rovan was the bed of many. Near him was the raising of Flaian's spear. Strong was the shield which opposed the fair-haired youth: The efforts of his few years against it were fruitless. His steel returned from the strength of Lochlin's warrior, like the falling drop that is dashed from the mighty rock, when its lofty cliffs are at war with the reigning blast. Its sudden journey is downwards. The earth is its tomb; and it shall no more rise on the wings of other storms.

Scarlaw saw the fall of his son: The strength of many rushed to his sword. The foe trembled at the raising of his steel. Swanvil *, the hero of other lands, held the shield to oppose it. Terrible was the meeting of the two chiefs! Earth rolled from the wreck of their footsteps:

Rocks

* This Swanvil appears to have been a great warrior. He makes a fine appearance in the poem which immediately follows this.

Rocks shook with the strength of their struggling. Trees forsook their roots, and hurried down before the course of their strife. Warriors saw it; and their spears ceased to rise.—Thy arm was strong, O Swanvil! and thy soul was bright; but who could withstand the might of Scarlaw?—The son of the distant land sank before it.

Who is he that is foremost on the south brow of the battle? His wings of steel are spread like the eagle, when she grasps the rolling cloud in her feathered bosom. The foe bends beneath his shield as the heath bends before the whirlwind, when the fold of the cloud is the bed of a hundred ghosts.—Who should it be, but Dowran from Morcraig's woody streams? The spear of his father is in his hand: Below is the bed of the mighty. Quick are the steps of the hero amongst the foe! He spares the feeble as he goes. Now he meets a shield of strength. The spears of the feeble, whom he passed, come behind. The glittering steel of the warrior rises no more. Mournful is the sound of his fall to Albin's race!—What breast did not sigh? What sword
was

was not forth? What spear did not rise for the fallen hero?—The steps of warriors were deep in blood: The collected strength of Albin was in the point of their swords.—The sons of Lochlin fled.

Pursue not the retiring foe, said Scarlaw: Enough of Lochlin's race lies behind. Come near, remaining strength of Albin, let us view our friends that are low. Where is Dowran, Feyglen's warlike son? I saw his forward steps in the bloody field; but my eyes meet him not here.

He lies on the south brow of the battle, said a warrior. The broken spear is in his hand: His shield is the bloody bed of his breast.

Alas! said the chief, too soon has the fate of the warrior met the hero. The sound of Albin's victory shall reach his father; but no son of his shall carry it. A feeble hand will carry back his shield; for the mighty arm that brought it forth, shall no more return.—O Dowran, chief of warriors! thy steps in battle were fierce as the course of the angry storm, when the tallest daughters of the wood bend before the strength of the rushing blast. But the

the shining of thy armour shall be no more seen in the fields of death. The swords of the mighty may rise; but thy shield will not oppose the coming storm. The foes of Albin will no more tremble at thy approach: No more shall thy arm be the shield of thy father's gray hairs.

A warrior sighed young Flaian's name. He is not here, said the chief: He lies amid the fallen sons of Lochlin. The strength of his arm failed; but my son is not alone. He was not backward in the battle. His arm would have been strong; but he fell like the young plant of Coil. The storm came round it before the spreading roots gathered strength: The blast of the north frowned on its tender leaves; and it sank, while trees of many years defied the storm.

O Flaian, where are the steps of thy speed, which were wont to bring thee forward in the chace!—They are no longer thine, early sunbeam! Too soon hast thou retired to thy narrow dwelling. But the stone of fame shall exalt its head, and tell to other years thy fall in the season of thy beauty. The virgins shall
view

view it; and the tear of pity shall glisten on their cheek, like the early dew on the opening rose. The stranger, as he passeth, will ask, ' who lies below?' Then will he hear of thy fall in the morning of thy days; and a sigh will come forth. The warriors of former years will look down from their bed of rest in the land of clouds, and rejoice. They will smile on thy tomb *, as they pass it on the wings of the blast, when their journey is in the storms of the nights of winter.—

The glittering of youthful warriors came round the smoaking spear of the chief. He wiped the tear from his eye, when he beheld their future battles.—But Dalay stood distant from

---

* It was the policy of the antients to persuade mankind, that those who fell in battle, were happy in a future state. This opinion was of infinite advantage, in acquiring or defending property, as it served to promote a ferocity of courage, in which the Christians themselves seem by no means to be defective. The leaders of each party have piously promised their followers happiness hereafter, as a just reward for the commission of murders and devastations, and inflicting the greatest miseries on their brethren of the human race.

from the reft, in the anguifh of his foul. He mourned the weaknefs of his arm, which brought him not forward in the battle.—He was behind; but fhields of ftrength oppofed the hero. The chief faw the downward face of his mourning, as he leaned upon his half-erected fpear. Warriors talked of the weight of their fteel; but the words of Dalav were not heard.

Son of my youth! thy back was not to the foe: Why then doft thou turn it upon thy father?—I faw the broken fhields round the rifing of thy fpear, and the days of my ftrength rufhed upon my foul. Why fhould my frowns be towards the hopes of my age? What tho' the fon of Feyglen has fallen; a feather has alfo dropt from Scarlaw's wing of ftrength.— Flaian fhall never more purfue the footfteps of the ftag, nor raife the fpear againft the foe. —But more fons are mine:—Albin will yet rejoice in their ftrength when I am low.

Never fhall Albin rejoice when thou art low, faid Dalav: It is from thy fword alone that her foes retire. We raife the fpear in vain: In vain does the wrath of our fteel attack the foe.

foe. Still are we behind: But thou conquereſt, and we come forward.

Thou ſtaidſt behind, my ſon; not that thine arm was feeble, but becauſe the foe was ſtrong.—But let us view our friends behind, that no ſon of Albin may ſleep without his fame.

Gillion, old warrior, thou art low!—No feeble arm has brought thee down.—Thou wert of thoſe that beheld the battles of my youth.—But the days of my youth ſhall no more return; nor thy ſpear, O Gillion! ever riſe in the fields of death. The foes that ſank before thee, were not of the feeble: The broken ſhields around thee fell not from the hands of little men.—Ye who have fought near me in the days of my youth, Why have ye left me alone? Ye are gone, my friends; and I ſtand, like the oak of Slimora, the only remaining daughter of the foreſt. Time! how haſt thou diſpoſed of her ſiſters, which once reared their haughty heads around her? They wave not now their verdurous branches near. No friendly oak ſhields her from the fury of the ſtorm. She has ſurvived all her friends. The blaſted trunk hangs its leafleſs boughs in ſorrow.

row.—Daughter of years, thy fall is near! Thou shalt soon be low; and the stream that bathes thy feet, shall pass over thee.

A young warrior appeared in batle.—I have been too late, O chief! but the foe may yet return. My arm is not strong; but I will fight beside young Flaian of the golden locks.

The strength of thy arm will increase, son of youth! said the chief: But Flaian will never lift the spear of battle. Retire to the hall of thy fathers, lest thou fall, like him, in the midst of thy blooming years.

The daughter of Feyglen heard his words. —She heard;—but withstood them not.—The shield dropt from her smooth arm:—She fell, and the clashing steel sounded round her white bosom.—The tear of the chief was seen;—the sigh of warriors was heard.—Heroes shook their heads in awful grief: Silent stood the darkened host. They saw the daughter of the chief of Feyglen; and their breath came mourning from the house of woe. A warrior said, ' her brother too has fallen.' The virgin opened her eyes:—A groan was heard. Dalav gently raised the swan-bosomed maid: He

raised

raised her with the hand of friendship. The thoughts of his breast had been before of her; but he knew not that the eyes of her love were towards Flaian.—

Give, O son of Scarlaw! said the maid,—give me the sword of Flaian. I will clasp it in my arms in the season of sleep; when my dreams are of him who raised it in battle.—

He gave her the sword.—She kissed the bloody steel.—The bed of its point was her bosom: Her own hand gave the wound.—She fell on the breast of Flaian.—One stone is their tomb.

THE

CHIEF of FEYGLEN*.

THE gray-haired chief of Feyglen leaned to the tree of the ruſtling leaf. The ſpear of his fathers was not near. It roſe high

---

* Feyglen, *the valley of deers.*—The ſubject of this poem is the ſame as the laſt; and, is ſuppoſed by ſome, to have been compoſed by the ſame bard. This, however, does not appear to be the caſe. There is a great difference in the manner of both poems in the original. The ſcarcity of terms in the Engliſh to expreſs the feelings of grief, martial atchievements, and other incidents with which this poem abounds, contributed much towards deſtroying this difference of manner in the tranſlation.

The moſt probable account which tradition gives of the author of this poem, is, that he was family-bard to the chief whoſe name it bears. He was ſo much affected with the diſtreſſes of his patron, that he took no further notice of the battle deſcribed in the preceding poem, than it was connected with the tragical fall of the houſe which is the ſubject of this

high in the hands of Dowran againſt Lochlin's race, iſſuing in hoſtile pride from the boſom of the troubled waves.

The golden-haired father of the morning came forth from the back of the eaſtern hill: He came forth in the ſteps of his beauty. The retiring clouds of night fly in haſte from the coming of his glittering beams. The feathered ſons of the foreſt rejoice in the kindneſs of his ſmiles. The ſoft heaving boſom of the mountain-lake, receives with joy the image of his beauty. The courſe of feeble waves is towards the trembling brightneſs. They ſalute it as they paſs; and leave it to adorn the ſurface of ſucceeding waves *.

The rolling of thy dim eyes, O chief of battles! is alſo towards the riſing ſun; but their darkened courſe is along the gloomy vale of black-robed night. The ſmiling beams of the morning are on thy gray hairs; but thine eyes of age behold them not. Darkneſs is before thee; but thy ſoul is the ſeat of light. The feats of former years revolve in the mind of

---

* No paſſage in the preſent collection has loſt ſo much in the tranſlation, as this deſcription of the ſun ſhining on a lake in a clear morning.

of the hero. The heart of the warrior is great with the deeds of other battles.

Where, said the chief, ah! where are the days of my youth, when I grasped the shield of my fathers, and was first in the strife of battles? When the ghosts of the mighty were behind, and the retiring foes of Albin before the glittering of my steel? When my spear was the shield of the feeble, and my sword the terror of the sons of ocean? My joy was then in the sound of Morven's battles, when the race of strangers raised spears of strength against her sons. But now the steel of foes is high, and I oppose it not. Morven calls her sons to battle; but my steps are not towards the foe. My feeble arm grasps no child of the furnace. My darkened eyes direct not the course of my footsteps. Lonely I sit beneath the tree of the trembling leaf!

Let the spear of my fathers be a meteor of death in thy hands, O Dowran, son of my youth! Be thou the shield of thy father's fame; and let the falling of my gray hairs rejoice in the sound of thy battles.

Who

Who comes in the noise of the rustling heath? Are thy steps from the strife of heroes? Stop the foot of thy speed, son of haste, and tell how warriors fought. Was Dowran forward in the bloody contest? Were his steps among the broken shields of the foe? Did spears of strength sink before him? Fled the mighty from the weight of his steel? Speak, tongue of the tale; for the darkened eyes of Feyglen behold no more the deeds of heroes.

As the rolling of the huge stone down the haughty brow of Morcraig, when the affrightened flocks stretch every nerve to shun the coming danger, and the torn heath is round the whirling of its rapid journey; so bold, so strong, so terrible was the son of Feyglen, in the fields of death. The mighty saw the coming of his strength, and they sank beneath the weight of his sword. The feeble fled the danger they could not meet. Albin's sons rejoiced in his deeds as they filled his footsteps behind.

Such was the rolling of his might, when the shield of Swanvil met the point of his spear. Stop—said the chief of Lochlin; and let the collected

collected strength of thy arm be in the darting of thy lance. Strong is the shield before thee, and mighty is the arm that supports the glittering wing of steel. My sword triumphs not in the fall of little men. I mourn when feeble foes are before me. But thy fame is great, O warrior! Thy coming in battle is like the coming of a hundred streams, when their foaming journey is down the shaggy brow of the haughty rock. We have both been renowned; but a gray stone will lift its mossy head on the hill before the storms of other years. The hunter, as he passeth, will cry, 'Here the mighty fought.' If my sword becomes thine, send it, O warrior, to Savina. Her soft-rolling eye meets the rising sun on the plains of Tauron. The maid will pierce her bosom with the point, and our ghosts will rejoice in the land of clouds.

No steel from me shall pierce the bosom of the lovely, said Dowran. Yield, warrior, and return in safety to Savina. Her mild eye will view thee with joy, and bless the hand that spared thee in battle.

In vain haſt thou ſpoke, ſon of pride! Perſuaſive ſweetneſs is not thine.—Thy words are feeble, like the blaſt that holds a conteſt with a ſtubborn rock. Did the points of five hundred ſpears meet my ſhield; did the ſtrength of a hundred warriors raiſe each ſpear; did the meteors of death fly around me, as the fire of heaven, when burſting clouds roll in horror through the angry ſky;—yet would I not yield.

* Two blue ſteels roſe in wrath. Dowran ſtood alone. Many ſons of Lochlin came behind. A bloody ſtream was ſeen.—Swanvil ſtopped the unequal ſtrife. The thoughts of the valiant darted on his ſoul. He curſed the coward's ſpear!

Dowran

---

* *Le naithes dh'eirich da lann ghorm, &c.* This paſſage hath been admired in the original, as comprehending more ſubſtance in a certain number of words, than any other poem extant. I have endeavoured to imitate the ſhortneſs of the periods in the original, though I am conſcious that I have fallen ſhort of its dignity. The Galic reader, however, will find, that no idea hath been totally loſt, though but faintly expreſſed.

Dowran fell not alone. On either side they bleed. The spear is the pillar of his bloody side. His shield rolls on earth. Terrible are the threatening looks of the hero. The foe viewed, and trembled. Ghosts fled from the fallen around. Terrified, they mount the clouds that pass. We heard the warrior's groans. Too late we raised the spear. Many sank with the hero: The rest fled in haste. Swanvil scorned our strength. He sought the sword of Scarlaw. But what son of song can relate the meeting of the two chiefs! Rocks spoke the words of steel. The broken shield sank from Swanvil. His spear shall rise no more.—The race of Lochlin fled. The blast is their shield, as they mount the blue rolling waves.

The aged Feyglen listened in the anguish of his soul to the tale of woe. A tear wanders down his wrinkled cheek. He clasps his hands in grief. Many groans come forth.—Mournful are his words.

A blast has withered the plains. A cloud has darkened the sky.—Joy meet the soul of the valiant. Never shall the spear of my fa-
thers

thers rife in battle! I fhall vanifh, like a dim fhadow that wanders before the rays of the moon. No fon of mine fhall raife the huge ftone near my narrow dwelling. My name fhall ceafe to found in the years that approach. My departure fhall be as the blaft that flies unheeded over the mountains.—A fudden beam of comfort rufhes on my foul. Sulalin, image of her who was lovely! reach me thy white hand. Gather thy waving locks from the wind. Dry thy father's cheek with thy foft ringlets. A tear from thy blue eyes fhall bathe my memory on the mountains. A plant may rife from thy fide. The fpear of Feyglen may yet rife in battle.—A ray of comfort rufhes on the wretched. Forgot I fhall not be, foft beam of youth!

The chief ftretched forth his hand. But he ftretched it to the wind.—No white arm received it: No foft voice was heard.—A blaft that withers rufhed through his nerves. He trembled as a feeble twig before the haughty ftorm. Breeze after breeze faluted the woods; but the gray-haired Feyglen liftened in vain.

—The

—The soft voice of Sulalin is not mingled with the wind.

A black cloud is gathering in the east. Why do the oaks bend their green heads before it? Why do the rocks rear their cliffy brows to meet it in wrath?—A hundred sighs are heard, as it flies in surly speed over the mountains. The tears of heroes pour forth before it. The death of the lovely has darkened its gloomy aspect. The fold of the cloud is the wing of a tale of woe.

Bathe thy dim eyes in tears, chief of the aged locks!—She who was bright in thy hall, sleeps cold in death. The ghost of the virgin rose on the fairest beam of the morning. The son of Scarlaw is the partner of her flight to the land of clouds. Piercing are thy words, son of the mournful tale.—But the eyes of Shearvan have already shed all their tears: His feeble breast hath already poured forth all its sighs. The rocks of Ardven have heard it, and returned their groans of pity.—But thou travellest in thy mirth, O son of heaven! regardless of my woes. And long mayest thou rejoice in thy blue fields, thou brightest tenant of the sky! The children of an hundred glens look with the eye of expectation for the coming forth of thy beauty, though the darkened eyes of Shearvan refuse to admit thy beams. But some day, like me, they will look in vain. Stormy clouds will wrap thee in their dark folds, when the battles of many ghosts are in thy land. Thou wilt then, like me, weep; but the wrathful winds will not regard thee.

But roll on, in all the strength of thy brightness, fair-haired traveller of the sky! Carry with thee all thy smiles to cheer the valiant who sleep in the Isle of Peace. The course of thy speed all day is towards them. The angry storms terrify not thee. Sullen clouds may veil thy beauty; but they cannot oppose thee. The couch of thy repose is with the ghosts of our fathers. There thou layest down thy fair head to rest; and the feeble children of the wind sleep among the golden locks of thy beauty.

O Sulalin! when other ghosts are asleep, steal thou in secret to the dreams of thy father. Tell me if Culoina has forgot me in the season of my gray hairs; she who had seen me in the days of my strength. But my strength is fled, like a blast to the desart: My friends have vanished as the mist on Ardven. Heavy are mine eyes of age! leave me to my rest, ye tenants of the hills.—Come, Sulalin! to the dreams of my slumbers.

Such were the words of the chief in the season of his woe. The voice of his grief was heard no more: His sighs ceased to mingle with the wind. His tomb lifts its head high on Ardven. The traveller listens to his tale with streaming eyes :—For he fell, like the last tree of the forest, when no plant remains to tell the place where it stood.

THE

CAVE OF CREYLA*.

COLD was the blast from the regions of frost, and fatal proved the surly offspring of the north to the feeble reapers of the flowery field. Legions of insects perished by the poisonous breath of the reigning storm. The feathered songster stopped the warbling note at the frowning approach of the rude intruder.

The Father of light withdrew his circular presence beyond the southern hill. Feeble were his oblique rays, which, half intercepted, dimly

---

* Creyla, *the woody rock*, supposed to be one of the Grampian hills which still retains that name.

The scene of this poem is said to have been in that valley round the head of the river Spey, which is, at present, known by the name of Bha-dianach, or Badenoch, *the secure valley*.

dimly shone o'er the tops of the mountains. The congealer of the liquid stream, who annually retires beyond the northern ocean, further than the cleavers of the waves can trace his rapid flight, returned from his summer expedition. He now began to usurp his tyrannical reign, in the absence of the fire of brightness, whose presence he would have shunned with a speed equal to his who flies from impending destruction. Nature trembles at the approach of the cruel spoiler; and the feeble among her sons fall victims to the resistless oppressor. He locks up the stream from the shaggy tenants of the forest; and the finny inhabitants of the flood dwell in darkness, while in vain they search for the intercepted day.

Such was the season, and dismal was the visage of the mountains, when Liachan led his six sons to the cave of Creyla. The frozen offspring of the sky had closed up the unfrequented entrance: But an impending cliff, which projected from the mother rock, contended with the passing blast; and the murmuring noise pointed out the door of the cave

* Lia-chean, grey head.

to the trembling leader of the youthful band.

Thrice did Liachan bless the lonely cavern as he entered, and thrice did the flinty pillars of the rock, with their echoing voices, return the friendly salutation through the hollow centre. The well-known cave recalled to the remembrance of the sage the companions of his youth, when he retired from danger to this gloomy cell. A deep sigh issued from his aged bosom, when his mind rolled back to the deeds of other years. He dropt the tear of affection to the memory of his departed friends.

Ranal, the last born son of his father, the swift ascender of the hill, misconstruing the cause of the trembling tear, opened his mouth, and pronounced the words of comfort to his disconsolate sire.

Why dwells muteness on the tongue, which was wont to claim attention, when the formers of the ring round the burning ourd, * harkened

---

* The ourd is the trunk of a large tree set on fire, round which the Highlanders solemnize particular festivals; a custom rigidly observed at this day, in many parts of the Highlands,

kened to the words of inſtruction? Welcome was the lovely offspring of thy mouth to the liſtning croud. Even the venerable bard, the ruler of the human heart, increaſed his knowledge, when he lent the ear of attention to the manly ſtrains which iſſued from the lips of Liachan. Why then ſits the emblem of remorſe on the brow on which the induſtrious propagators of ſlander could not trace the image of guilt? If the trembling viſage of fear, which was wont to be a ſtranger to thy breaſt, has paid thee an unaccuſtomed viſit, ſpurn from thy boſom with a ſmile the ungracious gueſt. Though thy feeble hand cannot graſp the weapons of reſiſtance, ſtrong ought to be that arm which unſheathes the ſword to attack

Highlands, where the ourd is annually provided for Chriſtmas eve, and the firſt night of the new year. Some traditions in the Galiç language repreſent this cuſtom as a monument raiſed from the ruins of barbariſm, and inform us, that the fire-wood which the ſons of cruelty were accuſtomed to provide, in the days of idolatry, to ſacrifice human victims to imaginary deities, was afterwards happily converted into the ourd, to raiſe the voice of mirth in the hall, while the bards ſung the deeds of heroes.

tack thee; for none of Liachan's sons, in the hour of danger, ever purchased their safety by retreat.

Stop, Ranal, said Liachan, these tears are not the offspring of fear; thou art a stranger to the cause. Thy sympathising eyes shall also yield their tributary drop, as soon as thou knowest the source from which they flow. The tale is unknown on the banks of the Tay *. I have wrapped it up with the finger of secrecy, till the nerves of my children gained strength to redeem their just rights by the glittering son of the furnace. Draw hither, my sons, and listen with the ears of attention to the unfeigned words of Liachan. Learn from them to avoid the follies of youth; so shall the tears of age never bedew your wrinkled cheeks.

But first let the spark of thy steel, Callan, dispel the gloom of the cave. Stop thou the speed of the stag, Ranal. The oaks of Creyla are many: Let a withered trunk blaze before me. But spare the feeble plant: Let the youthful branches wave in the wind. The summer's

* *Tath* from *Fladh*, the kindly stream.

summer's sun will yet return, and smile upon their tender leaves. The bounty of the spring will increase their strength; and warriors yet unheard of, will rejoice round their flames in distant years.—

The arrow of Ranal pierced a stag. The sword of Callan brought the fire from the rock.--Trees fell before Aspar; and why should Altban, Duchan, and Ogier, be forgot? —They were not idle.

Long had the frowning visage of darkness been the gloomy tenant of the cave: But the flaming breath of the oaks now expelled the ungracious intruder. A smile shone on the flinty cliffs. The chief viewed them, and sighed. —The image of the lovely half-appeared. He thought of the beam that had set.

In vain, says Callan, have we spread the feast: In vain hath the friendly oak blazed before thee. Thy dim eyes wander o'er the cave in sorrow: The tear of woe comes glittering forth.

And let them come, said Liachan.—The drop on one cheek bathes the memory of thy mother:

mother: The offspring of the other eye is for the fate of him, who has no son to warm his cave in the days of his gray hairs.—The storms that travel o'er the mountains reach not me. Your friendship hath spread joyful smiles round my cave; but cold is the seat of him who hath lost his sons in the days of his youth.

I ask for light, and it shines:—He asks for light, and darkness is around him. My stag lies by the flame of my oaks: His stag flies abroad in the forest. No son of his pursues it with the footsteps of speed.—I am warm, and the assiduity of my sons is round me; but he is cold, and his pale cheek leans against a pillar of ice—Alas, son of age! wert thou near, my children should warm thy cave also.——

The arm of my father Tomduth was the shield of my feeble years. In safety I rose behind it, like the tender shrub that rears its soft head near the stately oak. The blast on either side frowns in vain: The strength of many years meets it. The course of its flight is backwards, and the sound of its wrath is heard

heard on distant rocks. So fled the foes of Inver * from the sword of Tomduth.

As Trombia † in her hollow bed gathers her liquid strength from the fertile nerves of a thousand crystal rills, extending their winding arms round the heathy mountains; so gathered the evening the flocks of Tomduth to the plains of Elian.

The meeting of warriors was in the hall of Inver. Benvel ‡ struck the harp to the fame of departed heroes, and implanted the image of valour in the vacant breast of the rising generation. Hospitality stood at the outer gate, and with the finger of invitation waved to the traveller as he passed on his way. The chief stood unequalled in wisdom and valour. The venerable bard raised his voice to proclaim it. But where is the strength of the chief? Where the music of the bard?—Tomduth lies unactive

* *In-bher* signifies a place where a lesser river joins a greater, or empties itself into the ocean. All the towns in Scotland, whose names begin with *Inver*, are thus situated, as *Inver-ness, Inver-ary, Inver-keithing,* &c.

† *Trom-bidh, heavy stream,* a river which owes its birth to a lake in the valley of Gauig, and empties itself into the Spey, a little below Ruthven.

‡ Bein-bheal, *sweet voiced.*

active in the tomb of Killmore *. Eternal muteness reigns on the quivering tongue of Benvel. The father of the song shall no more be heard at the feast of Balden †.

The chief retired not like a misty cloud before the face of the blast. He foresaw his fall; and his son received the words of instruction.

Liachan, I am old.—The meteors of death have warned me to depart ‡. I go to visit the

---

* *Cill* signifies a place of interment. St Andrew's is at present known by no other name in the Galic than Cill-ribhen, *the royal burial place.*

† The modern Beltane is but a corruption of this word. The feast was kept on the first day of summer. A particular kind of bread used at it, is still made in several parts of the Highlands at this day. The leaven, before it is fired, is spread on both sides with a liquid, composed of yolks of eggs, sweet cream, butter, &c. If any family neglects to use this bread, on that day, it is positively asserted, that their flocks will diminish that year; and several precedents are produced to authenticate the fact.—So effectually has superstition consecrated this custom

‡ The inhabitants of different parts of the Highlands give different accounts of these meteors of death. The most curious are those of the people round the river Spey. The meteor here does not, as in other places, appear like fire

the ghosts of our fathers. Come to the rocks of Creyla: Receive an aſylum ſacred to the chief of Inver.

The warrior was bright in the armour of his fathers: But the liquid ſons of ſorrow ruſhed to my eyes, and concealed him from my eager view. My throat denied a paſſage to the thoughts of my breaſt; they were big, and could only find their paſſage by halves. Words, at laſt, were formed from the broken accents. —We

fire flying in the air; but is heard with a feeble voice, ſlowly traverſing the path which the funeral is to paſs, and is called *Tachran*. Perſons are ſaid to be deaf to the noiſe of their own Tachran, though others hear it ſo diſtinctly, that they can trace its progreſs to the houſe from which the funeral is ſoon to proceed.

The Tachrans are very different from the ghoſts, as they are never known to do any harm; for, if a perſon purſues them, they always retire.

Perſons, whoſe veracity cannot be called in queſtion in other matters, relate unaccountable ſtories concerning them, to which they declare themſelves to have been witneſſes.—This furniſhes an inſtance of the unbounded power which ſuperſtition maintains over the mind; and diſplays the force of that rhetoric by which ſhe perſuades the human race to become her votaries, in whatever preposterous garb ſhe chuſes to appear.

—We passed thro' the glen of Elian.—The wind of the north came rushing o'er the heath, and rattled on the armour of Tomduth as it passed: The armour of Tomduth regarded it not; and we reached the cave of Creyla, as if quietness had been the ruler of the night.

Tomduth was tall: He leaned upon his half-erected spear as he entered. The spear saluted the threshold. Fire fled the daughter of the rock, at the embrace of the steel. The flinty sisters of the cave echoed a chorus to the sound, to welcome the chief, the only visitor of the lonely cell.

This cave, said Tomduth, is hitherto unknown to the sons of the heath. Let it protect the feeble of thy race, if thy foes shall urge the contest; but seek not thy own safety in concealment. Fly not in the face of danger; nor tremble when the meteors of death are around thee. Be not the first to draw, nor the first to sheath the sword. Avoid not the combat with the mighty; but shun the ignoble contest. Let thy face be to the strong, and thy back to the feeble foe.

Make

Make not the daughter of Dungeal * the mother of thy sons. Poison not the offspring of thy loins by mingling in their composition the juice of a baneful plant. Let the milky food of their infant days be derived from a pure fountain: So shall they be defended from the weeds which corrupt the heart.

The words of instruction were ended; and the daughters of the rock ceased to enforce the precepts of the chief. Muteness was in the cave; and nought was heard but the voice of night, which in hoarse accents saluted the rocks as it passed.

The tomb of the chief rose on Killmore: Benvel's song of woe was heard round the ourd. The tear of beauty bedewed the cheek of the virgin: Warriors shook their dejected heads as they met. Rocks joined in pity the sound of grief: Each breeze was the messenger of a tale of woe.

Stormal

---

* Dun-geal, *white tower*.—The house of Dungeal are said to have been the progenitors of the Cummings, lords of Badenoch, whose transactions are so well known in the history of Scotland.

Stormal was the stately son of Dungeal. He led the warriors of his father to battle. The arrow of random fled not from his bow. She continued her journey to the distant mark; and fatal proved her arrival to the breast of the foe.

Sulgorma * was the feat of a thousand beauties. Many heroes wooed the maid; but the thoughts of her dreams were of Liachan, though I regarded not the kindly glances of her blue eyes.—So look the wishing eyes of the bewildered traveller in search of the intercepted beams, when the loaded sky leans her burden of mist on the hills of Minaig. But the ungrateful tenant of the enlightened vale views, with eyes of indifference, the bountiful favours of the Father of light.

The feast of Balden was spread at Dungeal. Bards sung the tales of love.—I forgot the words of instruction, and opened my eyes to the beauties of Sulgorma. I looked in kindness on the maid, and saw her clothed in loveliness. Our meetings were often in secret, and
we

* Sull-gorm, *blue-eyed.*

we thought of each other in the season of dreams.

Benvel saw my love for Sulgorma, and the friendly resentment of his breast awaked.——— Son of Tomduth, said the bard, departed is the fame of thy house! The words of instruction thou hast regarded as the blast that flies o'er the mountains.- Luachos, of the race of bards, bring my harp, and place my partner in danger by my side. I will wander to other lands. Too long hath my song been heard at Inver.

Son of the days of old, said I, weighty are thy words. Feeble is the breath of unripened years; and fruitless are her efforts when arrogantly she endeavours to oppose the offspring of thy mouth. Thy tongue has given birth to piercing words; but Liachan stands reproved by the frowns of friendship. Were the beauties of Sulgorma as the sun of heaven in the infancy of day, never should she shine in the hall of Inver.

Malalin * of the graceful eye, the beautiful daughter of the chief of Ervin, mourned the fall

* Mal-alin, *graceful eye-brow.*—Er-bhin, *western hill.*

fall of her father. The emblem of grief sat on her cheek. I blessed the maid of woe, and brought her to the hall of my fathers.

Stormal heard the secret sigh of Sulgorma, and raised his threatening spear. Many were his warriors, and weighty was his sword in the day of death. I gathered the strength of Inver to oppose him; but feeble proved my arm in every contest; for my spear was raised against an injured foe.

Many were the years of our strife; and many the deaths of our warriors. When the force of Inver failed, I brought Malalin to the cave of Creyla *. The safety of my sons was her care. I slew the deer of the desart, and carried them to our feast.

But, blessed be the soul of her who feasts no more in my cave!—When the daughter of Ervin retired to the land of ghosts, I carried my sons to the tower of the woody vale, by the

side

* It was customary for every great family to have a secret cave, or place of concealment from their enemies, when they were forced to fly in battle. The vestiges of some of these caves are still to be seen; but, when once they became known, they were of no further use.

side of the friendly stream. There Gildea *
wiped the tear of grief from mine eye. My
sons rose like the young plants of the forest.
Their hills are many round the streams of
Speymore; and their arms are now strong to
fight the battles of Inver against the intruding
race of Dungeal.

* Of Gill *a servant*, and Dea *God*.—The *Gillindea*, i. e. *servants of God*, mentioned in antient poetry, is the true origin of what was afterwards corrupted, by writers who understood not the language, into *Kelledei*, or *Culdees*.

An explanation of some firnames in Scotland will put the truth of this beyond a doubt. Gilchrist, *Christ's servant*; Gilespie, *the Bishop's servant*; Gilmore, *the great servant*, &c.

COLMALA

COLMALA AND ORWI.[*]

WHY does the tear of woe trickle down the wrinkled cheek of Chrimor?—Often has the stranger feasted in his hall; when the shell of mirth went round, and bards sung the warriors of other days. His friends are many in other lands, but mournful is the chief. His mighty son sleeps among the waves, and the soul of the aged is sad.—

Colmala and Orwi, the maids of the hill of hinds, were clothed with loveliness: The locks of their beauty flew on the wings of the wind. White was the heaving of two fair bosoms behind their polished bows. Often had they led their father's hounds to the chace; for the old hero sat lonely in his hall, and mourned the fall of all his sons.

[*] Col-mhalla, *small eye-brow.*—Or-bhiedh, *yellow locks.* Chri-mor, *great soul.*—Fer-guth, *the man of the word.*

Many warriors followed the daughters of beauty to the chace, and poured forth their sighs in secret. But warriors sighed in vain; for one was their love, and stately was he! the mighty son of Chrimor. The friendly beams of both their soft eyes were towards the hunter; but fixed was his love on Colmala, the maid of the raven locks.

Daughter of my father, said Orwi, thou love of Fergus! death is at my heart I feel it there, my friend.—Wilt thou raise a tomb o'er the unhappy?—My father is old, and thou art the choice of my hunter. He will, perhaps, aid thee, and give a stone. So shall Orwi sleep in peace; nor shall her pale ghost wander among the clouds of stormy night, when the north pours its frozen venom on the lifeless plains.

Alas! Orwi, thou sister of my love, why so pale?—What shall Colmala do, to draw death from thy bosom?—Thou must not fall in the strength of thy beauty, thou graceful bearer of the bow!

But soon shall I cease to bear the bow.— My life is in the mountain-ash, that rears its lofty

lofty head on sea-surrounded Tonmore*. The crimson fruit of the red-haired tree is in bloom. One branch would save the life of Orwi:—But no hunter is her's, and the sons of little men shun the isle of death with horror:—No brother of love to raise his white sails, and bring life to Orwi over the waves.—I fall unheeded on the plain: Raise the tomb of the unhappy, thou sister of Orwi!

Yes, Orwi! thy tomb shall rise:—But the son of thy son shall raise it. A red haired branch of the mountain-ash shall travel over many

---

* Tonn-mor, *the isle of great waves*, is said to have been one of the Orcades, then in the possession of the Norwegians. The inhabitants had been told by their bards, that, if strangers saw the beautiful berries of their mountain-ash, they would thereby be tempted to invade their country; and, with a pretension to foreknowledge peculiar to the times, assured them, that, if a branch of it was carried from their island, they should be no longer a people. The populace, always liable to be deceived, and ever ready to enlist under the banner of superstition, saw clearly the propriety of this prediction; and, in the heat of enthusiastical zeal, took precautions against it in a more austere manner, than perhaps the bards at first intended, by killing every stranger who came to the island.

many feas to the maid of the yellow locks. Fergus lifts the fpear of the mighty; and he will bring it from the ifle of death.

Colmala bore the groans of Orwi to the youth of her love. He fighed for the fickly maid:—He called his warriors from his hundred glens. The fons of battle grafped their maffy fwords. He rufhed in the ftrength of his dark fhips into the blue plains of ocean; and raifed the fpreading wings of his fpeed before the wind. Many feas he paffed; and the joy of his foul was great when the ifle of Tonmore rofe on the top of the waves.

Whence is the fpeed of the ftrangers, faid Anver, the gloomy chief of Tonmore?

From Innif-gaul *, the land of many ifles, we come.—A mountain-afh bends over thy rocks: The fame of the red-haired plant has travelled over many feas. The life of a virgin is in the tafte of the crimfon fruit. Yield a branch to the maid of woe, thou chief of
Tonmore;

---

* Innis-ghaull, *the iflands of ftrangers*. The weftern ifles are, at this day, known by that name in the Galic. The ftrangers here alluded to, are the Danes, who appear to have been in poffeffion of thefe ifles for fome centuries.

Tonmore; and the mighty shall be thy friends in the woody straths of Albin.

In vain have ye passed o'er many seas, ye sons of Innis-gaul! Did the strength of all your land appear, the strength of all your land were in vain. No branch of the sacred tree shall ever travel to the land of strangers. Unhappy are they who ask it:—Never more shall they return to the hall of their fathers. Unhappy are ye, sons of the sea; for never more shall ye raise your white wings of speed.—Bring my sword of the heavy wounds.—Gather my warriors with their spears of strength. —Raise the sign of death on Luman. Let the sons of the strangers fall in their blood.

Fergus raised his terrible voice; nor silent stood the rocks of Tonmore. They foresaw the death of their people, and the sigh of woe issued from the hardest flint.—But pleasant are the words of the chief to the rising wrath of his faithful warriors.

Ye have heard the words of the surly: My friends! we are in the land of death. Shall we sink like the harmless roe before the spear of
the

the hunter? Shall we fall like the tender lily of the vale before the blast of the north?—Yes, my friends, we may fall: But the aged chief of Strathmore shall not blush for his people.

Then Fergus raised his bossy shield, and shook his spear of death. His warriors gathered around, like a rock that gathers strength to meet the storm. The sons of Tonmore fell in blood. The spear of Fergus was a meteor of death. The surly king shrunk from its wrath.—Fly to thy gloomy hall, thou leader of the feeble! Fergus scorns thy death;—it would darken his battles.

The chief of Tonmore is overcome, and bound: His people are dispersed.—The mountain-ash falls on the plains of death. Ten warriors bear it to the dark ships of Fergus.—He raised his wings of speed. The wind came from the north; but it came in wrath, and aroused the sable surges from their sullen sleep.

The tear of the cloud flies on the blast: Waves rear their green heads to meet it. The fire of heaven darts over the waves. The

battles

battles of ghosts are in the sky. Liquid mountains raise their white locks before the wrath of the storm: Brown rocks gather strength to meet them. Proud billows spend their rage on the cliffy shore: Their retiring groans are terrible. The peasant hears it, and rejoices in his safety. The stag starts by times from his heathy couch. The eagle dreams of his fluttering prey. The cropers of the flowery field are half awake. The drousy eye-lids of the feathered flock are open. Half-extended, wings lean on the wind:—The dread of surrounding gloom prevents their flight.

The wearied storm now makes a pause.— Clouds lean their empty breasts on the mountains. Winds cease to roar, and trees to bend beneath their fury. The breath of night is silent. The waving heath now sleeps in peace, or trembles before the intermitting breeze.

The moon looks forth from the skirts of a dark cloud: The tear of the lovely glitters in the beam. Colmala mourns on the shore of the isle of oaks. Her long shadow wanders from rock to rock. Her raven-hair sighs in the gale: Her variegated garment flutters in the

the wind.—Two black eyes roll in forrow o'er the foaming deep; but the floating oak of her lover mounts not the rifing billows.

Blaſt followed blaſt. Cloud rolled on cloud. Star after ſtar went to reſt in the weſt. But no bold prow came cleaving the face of the deep.—A hundred times fancy faw the bark: A hundred times it proved a ſurge of ocean.

A fail at laſt reared its nodding head before the moon. A ſhadow rolls from wave to wave. Stars are hid behind its folds. A freſh-ning gale fwelled the fail, and added to its ſpeed.—The tear of the virgin ceafed. A beam of joy ruſhed on her foul :—She bleſſed the ſtrength of the oak.

A threatening rock raiſed its dark head: The furious waves are repelled. The wind is behind the bark: The rock meets it in wrath. —The fail nods no more.—A hundred fcreams are heard.—Colmala re-echoed the found. Her piercing cries rend the air: Her white bofom meets the flood. The lover can receive no aid; nor will the maid furvive him. Sea-wolves tear her beauteous limbs:—Her ghoſt
rufhed

rushed through the flood. Two dim forms rose from a wave; they mount a misty cloud. Often they return from their dwelling in the sky.—The mariner shuns with horror the rock of death, near the verge of ocean's wing *.

THE

---

* It was observed, in honour to the Caledonians, by a gentleman well acquainted with their antient poetry, that no private discord ever subsisted among the offspring of the same family. The present poem furnishes an instance to the contrary; as the destruction of Fergus, and disappointment of her sister, was the design of Orwi, whose subsequent history the bard passes over with that contemptuous neglect which her character deserves. In alleviation of this lady's crime, however, let it be remembered, that she is entitled to make the same defence so often made for others in her situation; she was in love, and disappointed. Although this apology cannot take off the odium with which her character is clogged, it places it in a more favourable light, than if she had been actuated by mercenary views.

THE OLD BARD's WISH*.

O PLACE me by the side of the murmuring rill, that gently glides with downward-rolling pace! Lay my head in the shade of the spreading branches, and be thy friendly beams, O sun! in kindness around me.—There at ease let my side embrace the green grass on the bank of the flowery garb, and let me taste the friendship of the breeze as it passes. Let my feet,

---

* Tradition does not pretend to give the name of the author of this poem.—Those who rehearse it, at present, in the Highlands, differ with respect to the arrangement. Compositions of a pastoral strain, are more liable to this confusion, than those of a narrative; as one part leads to another. The reader will find the present version different from that of Mr M'Donald's, who lately published the original in his collection of Galic poems; but the Translator has adopted that which appeared the most rational.

feet, bathed in the cryftal flood, feel the ftruggling efforts of the yielding ftream in its hafty journey.

Let the lily of pureft complexion fmile near me on the yielding ftalk; and the trembling dew glitter on the waving locks of my verdant feat. Let my hand recline on the daified turff, and let the fragrant thyme be the pillow of my leaning cheek.

Round on the high erected brows of my glen, let the hawthorn fpread its blooming boughs, and the little children of the bufhes rejoice in the fongs of their love, repeated by the invifible tenants of the rock.

Burfting from the opening jaws of the bird-haunted rock, let the new-born fpring fing melodious notes in a mournful tone; and let the hidden fons of the rock, from their hollow caverns, join the mufic of the founding ftream.

Let the variegated hills, and the wide extended dales, re-echoe the voice of the joyful flocks, while a hundred lowings are heard from the fides of furrounding vallies.

Borne

Borne on the wings of the paffing breeze, let the gentle voice of the fportive lamb falute my ear; and come, thou little kid, from the rocks, and fleep in fafety within the folds of my arms.

O let the hafty fteps of the hunter be near me, with the rattling noife of his darts, and his hounds rufhing along the extended heath! A beam of youth will glitter on my cheek, when the ftag-hunting noife fhall arife.

When the panting breath of dogs and youths is round me, the marrow of my bones will revive; and, when the fall of the ftag is proclaimed, my heels fhall leap in joy along the tops of the mountains.

Then fhall I meet the hound, my companion in the chace, when the rocks were wont to anfwer to the voice of the horn. I will enter the friendly cave, to whofe hofpitable door we bent our fteps at the approach of night.— Chearfulnefs fmiled round the gleam of our oaks: In the joys of our cups there was much mirth. The afcending fmoke was from the feaft of deer: Our drink from the ftream of Triga.

Triga *: Tho' ghosts had shrieked, and fairies screamed from their green hillocks, safe below the protecting roof of the cave, sweet was our repose.

What hill can vie with thee, O Beinard †, thou chief of a thousand hills! The dreams of stags are in thy locks. Thy head is the bed of clouds.

Scuralt rears his cliffy head near. The waving tops of a thousand green firs nod on his brows. The voice of the cuckow mingles with the soft blast that travels in kindness through the sky. The peasant hears it, and rejoices

in

---

* Triga, *the stream which forsakes the hills.*

† Bein-ard, *high mountain.*—The word *mountain* is used here not as a proper explanation of *Bein*, but because the English can furnish no better. That language discovers a great degree of poverty, when we examine those few terms it gives to the various convexities which appear on the surface of the earth. The Galic affords no less than nine names for hills, according to their different shapes and sizes, of which *Bein* is the loftiest. For these the English can only produce two, *hill* and *mountain*.

When objects of this nature frequently occur, there must be a *sameness*; and the bards, by these means, may be blamed for what is evidently the fault of the language into which they are translated.

in the returning smiles of summer. Early herbs shoot forth their green heads. Young roes gather strength. The elk majestic strides from hill to hill.

Half-formed waves travel along the smooth-faced lake below. Woody islands raise their green firs before them. The mountain-ash bends over the flood. The white-bosomed daughter of the stream mounts the soft billows: Her extended neck rises on the wandering waves. When she spreads her wings above the mountains, her flight is quick from cloud to cloud. Over boisterous seas she travels to other lands, where the cleavers of the wave never raised the swelling sail.

On what distant shore does the wind meet thy mournful song, son of my youth * ! Are thy

---

* This address of the bard to his absent son, is handed down with some difference. Several persons who rehearse the rest of the poem, omit this altogether. Others confuse it, by repeating it as altogether addressed to the swan. This mistake seems to arise from the similarity of sound in the two words *Ealla*, swan, and *Ghilla*, thou youth.—After the Translator had collected all he could, he found the passage still wrapped in obscurity: Tradition, however, pretends to throw some light on it.

The

thy tears for the fallen? Has the white armed daughter of beauty vanished before the eager glances of thy wishing eyes?—Peace round the tomb of the lovely!

Come forth from thy dark cave, voice of woe! The beam that is set shall not return. Rush from the womb of the rock. Gather thy floating oaks: Raise thy white wings of speed. Mount the high brows of the tumbling waves: Roll in swiftness before the strength of the travelling blast. Come to the banks of my lonely glen. Let me hear thy melodious song

The bard, who was himself a chief, had an only son, who fell deeply in love with Lavinia, the beautiful daughter of Thalbar. Lavinia was drowned as she was bathing in the lake of Triga. Morlav, the bard's son, becoming desperate, from the death of his mistress, sailed for the Orkney isles, hoping to fall in the wars of that prince, who was then at variance with the king of Norway. His valour and good conduct, however, gained him great fame; and, after the Norwegians were defeated and expelled the isles, the prince, in consideration of his services, and personal merit, offered Morlav his daughter in marriage, which he refused, and retired to a cave in a lonely isle, where his father heard he still continued to mourn his lost Lavinia.

THE OLD BARD's WISH.

song warbling in plaintive accents from thy breast of woe. Be thou on the tops of my mountains, and let the mournful tale of thy love be in thy mouth, O youth, who has travelled from the land of green waves! Pour forth thy luxuriant music in the bosom of the wind. Attention will seize my ears. I will snatch thy tale from the skirts of the fleeting cloud, when its misty journey is over the peaceful lake.

Tell me, for my sight is failed, O wind! where does the reed of the mournful sound raise its waving head? On what fertile mead is the gathering of its strength? Whistle among its locks as thou passest, friendly blast, and direct me to its dwelling.

Lend me thy aid, arm of strength! Place me before the kindness of the sun, when his darting favours are from the center of the azure arch. Spread forth thy broad wing, green-robed branch, and be the shield of my dim eyes from the fervour of the mid-day blaze. Then come, O memory of the past! in the likeness of a dream which travels in the season of stars. Come to the couch of my slumbers,

slumbers, and refresh me with the deeds of youth.

Behold, O my soul! yon beautiful maid, under the rustling wing of the oak, stately king of the forest! her white hand, the pillar of her glowing cheek, half-hid among the golden ringlets of her flowing hair. The darts from her swift rolling eye are towards the happy youth of her love. He leans on her bosom. She listens to his song in silence. The soft breeze from his mouth has raised a gentle tempest. White waves travel along the bosom of the virgin. Love flies from eye to eye. Deers stop their course on the heath. Their feet forget to move at the sound of the tale of love.

Now the song has ceased. The heaving of her white bosom meets the breast of her lover; and her lips, like the rose, blushing on the mead, are pressed by the happy youth.

Happiness without end to the tender pair, who have awaked in my mind a glimpse of those pleasures that shall not return! Joy to thy soul, lovely virgin of the soft-waving locks!

Hast

THE OLD BARD's WISH.

Hast thou forsaken me, happy dream? Return yet one transient gleam, O memory of the past!—But, alas, thou heardst me not. Sorrow rushes on my soul, like the winged blast that whistles in my aged locks.—Ye mountains who have seen my strength, farewell! Farewell, dear companions of my youth!—Ye virgins of the beautiful aspect, adieu! The joy of summer is yours; but my winter shall be everlasting.

O lay me near the hoarse voice of the falling stream, that tumbles in frothy haste from the cliffy brow; and let the last shutting of my eyes be softened by the soothing sound. Place my harp, and a full shell by my side; and let the shield that covered my fathers in battle be near.

Come, O cloud, that travels over many seas! Bear me on thy misty wings to the Isle of Peace, where the heroes of old nod their dim heads in awful slumbers. Open the hall where Ossian and Deal reside *; for the evening will come

---

* This passage furnishes an instance of the vanity to which every class of men is liable, when once the populace

come when the bard shall be no more. But, oh! before it comes,—before my ghost shall travel to Ardven, from whence there is no return, give me the harp, and the shell for the journey. Then, my beloved harp and shell, —then, farewell*!

lace profess themselves their disciples. The veneration which mankind entertained for the bards, encouraged that order to carry its pretensions of superiority to an extraordinary height. They imagined that a magnificent hall was appropriated for them in FLATHINNIS, to which no vulgar ghost could be admitted; and that they should there receive the rewards due to the strenuous exertion of their talents while on earth, to reclaim and cultivate the human race.—This opinion, if not rational, seems at least natural; for it has made its appearance among another class of men, who pretend to be directed by infallible rules.

* A palpable contradiction appears in this paragraph, which, however, a knowledge of the opinions of the antients will help to explain. It was imagined, that the ghosts of departed friends came to conduct the spirit of the deceased to *Flathinnis*. As these ghosts were supposed to be still susceptible of the pleasures which they enjoyed while on earth, music, and the liquor which they drank out of the shell, were provided in great plenty on these occasions, in order that they might take a sufficient quan-

tity

tity of food and mirth, to enable them to perform their journey to paradise with the more alacrity. If a deficiency was found in the entertainment, the ghosts were to be revenged on those whose business it was to have provided it properly. Thus it became sacrilege to have a funeral ill provided. The bard here desires the harp and shell to be ready to entertain his departed friends, and then bids them farewell, as he would have no further occasion for them.

DUCHOIL's

DUCHOIL's ELEGY.[*]

NO feeble voice is thine, son of death! No boy's staff is thy dart. The mighty overcome in battle; but they sink before thee. No shield can meet thy spear: No arm can oppose thy strength. All the heroes of former days have dropt into the grave at thy nod!

The mighty bend before thee with the feeble; but they shall not, like them, be forgot

---

[*] Duth-choil, *black wood*.—This chief is much celebrated by tradition for his hospitality to strangers, for whom he always kept open table. It is said, that such numbers came from Ireland to live on his bounty, that he was obliged, for obvious reasons, to make a law, that no stranger should continue on a visit longer than a year and a day, unless he could give a sufficient reason for it. During that space of time, any person had a right to demand entertainment, without even giving an account of himself; but, at the expiration of it, he behoved either to discover himself, or depart.—The M'Kenzies are said to be descended from this chief.

got by the voice of mid-night tale *. The sound of their fame shall mingle with the clouds that roll behind thee. Their tombs shall rear their gray heads, and wage a contest with the blasts of other winters.. The hunter will view the chace from their tops. The stag will shun the storm near them. The stranger will view them and sigh. The fame of the valiant shall travel to other lands.

But the little soul shall vanish, like the fleeting cloud, that wanders among the twinkling

---

* The mid-night tales here alluded to, are those rehearsed at late-wakes to entertain the people who sit up with the corpse. The desire of hearing those poems, draws together the inhabitants, from a great way round, who are so much captivated with the compositions, that they behold, with reluctance, the approach of morning. This custom owes its origin to the bards, who were wont, on such occasions, to relate the actions of the deceased. Hence, it became customary, on the death of such persons as were not entitled to eulogiums, to sing the deeds of antient heroes; and, as the audience naturally retained what had made such a deep impression on the mind, it has fortunately proved the great means of preserving some of the sublimest poems in the Galic language from the womb of oblivion.

ling stars. It shakes its misty garment on the mountains The course of a blast is towards it. Frightened at the fury of the wind, it disappears, and its dim form is no more remembered. The fair-haired morning shall rejoice in the east, and shall not meet it: The sun shall smile in the face of heaven, and shall not behold it.

Lately we looked, and, behold! the chief of Shirar strode in his might. The armour of his battles was near him. His strength was the shield of the feeble; his hall was the home of strangers †. The sons of other lands tasted

---

† If the reader is inclined to compare an antient to some modern chiefs, he may peruse the following lines translated from Dugal Bawn, composed about the time of the late emigration to America.

The pale-fac'd tenant of your cottage hears,
With heart-felt grief, the tales of other years.
What tho' his noble sire, with sword and shield,
Procur'd him freedom in the bloody field;
What tho' the father's arm the battle won?
No comfort reaches to the wretched son.
His much-lov'd wife and infants, pale thro' want,
Demand that succour which he cannot grant.
The youthful group around the mother hings,
And craves relief from hunger's piercing stings.

tasted his friendship: His fame traveled over many seas.—But this day's sun bears witness to a change, and has seen his fall, like the mighty oak, which had long shaken its bushy head above the forest. The ax of the hewer came in the day of its strength, and laid its spreading branches on the ground. Fly now unrestrained, noisy blast! No tall trunk rears its stately head to oppose thy rapid journey. Death came like a dark cloud from the north, that hides the sun behind its sable wings. The hills around are sad: The vallies mourn beneath

The mournful fair, with anguish, hears their cries,
The big tear gushing from her streaming eyes.
The trembling suns of woe perform in haste
Their rapid journey down her swan-like breast.
Her last-born suckling sips the briny flood,
And drinks grief's offspring with the milky food.
Sighs fought with words, and stopt their passage long,
While half-form'd accents perish'd on her tongue.
But fault'ring words at last made good their way.
O tho', &c.

The subject here becomes religious, which, in Galic poetry, is seldom worthy of imitation, as they received their system of it from a class of men who are no ways famed for liberal sentiments.

beneath its frowns. The liquid plains cease to glitter. The red deer couches below the elbow of the rock. Silence is in the wood. The feathered people shun the drop beneath the spreading leaves. The hound shakes his ears, and fills the footsteps of the home-bound hunter.

Many were the streaming eyes that viewed thy entrance into the narrow house, thou chief of battles!—Weep, ye maids of woody Fuarven! Mourn, ye youths of the hill of hinds! The chief of the people is low.

Who shall lead us in the day of strife? Where is the shield of our safety, when the foe appears?—The head of the glens is low: Feeble are the people without a leader.

Who is she that wanders with distracted steps on the mountains? What dark eye gives the tear of woe to the wind? What hand of snow strews the long dishevelled hair on the bosom of the breeze? What white bosom heaves to the blast in sorrow, and calls in vain to her hunter?—Who, but the daughter of generous Garven, could display such charms?

charms? Who, but the spouse of Duchoil, could pour forth such sighs?

Range in safety thro' his woods, ye dark-brown deer. The hounds of the chief are howling in his hall. Often they follow the tearful spouse of their master's love. And often shall you follow her in vain, ye faithful sons of swiftness! who were wont to outstrip the wind:—Never more shall Duchoil lead you to the chace!

The stranger from a-far shall come to the hall of the open door. He will ask for the chief of the stretched-forth hand; but the shaking head will answer with a silent tear. Then will he hear of thy fall, O chief of Shirar! and his sigh will come forth. He will mourn at thy tomb; but thou wilt not hear him †.— Alas! Son of the distant land, thy

---

† Most of these poems, especially those in the Elegiac strain, were generally rehearsed extempory. On that account they are frequently defective in point of connection, leaving the reader often abruptly, as in the present case. The idea of the strangers, who had formerly been entertained by the hospitable chief, mourning at his tomb, appeared so strong to the bard, that he concluded a description

thy words are piercing. Other clans dwell in safety under their chiefs; but the arm of our strength is low.

SUL-scription of it to be boyond his reach. He therefore leaves his audience to form to themselves this affecting scene. To a superficial reader, therefore, the most valuable passages must be lost, as they require a strenuous exertion of attention to which few will perhaps think them entitled.

No species of composition leaves greater room for the imagination to work upon, than the Celtic poetry. The bards were a class of men who became venerable from their gray hairs, as well as respectable from their profession. Destitute of every aid which literature furnishes for the improvement of the mind, they were under the necessity of gathering their knowledge from experience. Although this be the most infallible, it is by no means the most expeditious method of acquiring it; and a life must be far spent before much acquisition can be made. For this reason, the bards always appear old men. Thus, adorned with locks worn gray in the service of their country, and surrounded by some of those who had been witnesses to the atchievements of their youth, they delivered their sentiments, with that dignity of stile, and freedom of expression, which a mind conscious of its own superiority naturally claims; and mankind received whatever they advanced, without presuming to exercise the talents of criticism.

SULVINA's ELEGY.

COME forth, sigh of woe. Roll down, tears of grief. Mourn the fall of the lovely. Bathe the memory of the white-armed daughter of Morauld.

Why doth the wandering stream smile as it passeth? Why doth the finny tribe sport in the crystal flood? Roll in darkness, ye glittering waves! Retire to the blackest pool, ye silver-winged!

Sound no horn on my hills, ye followers of the stag! Spare the hide of the roe, ye bearers of the bow!

Nod your green heads in grief, ye leafy daughters of the forest! Sing a tale of woe, ye tenants of the bush!

Why dost thou travel in thy mildness, soft breath of summer? The fairest flower that ever met thee is low. The friendship of the breeze shall no more smile on the cheek of the rose. The waving ringlets of her dark-brown hair

hair shall no more tremble on the wings of the passing blast.

Away with thy voice of mirth, joyful morning! She, who was wont to shine before thy early beams, shall not awake. Hang your drooping heads, ye flowers of the mead! A surly blast has plucked the fairest lily from her stalk. Lonely is her dwelling in the gloomy tomb. The sun-beams of coming years shall not smile on her virgin-charms.

But come, O come, with all thy sable clouds, black-robed night! Grasp the hills in thy dark bosom. Let the shrieks of ghosts, the screams of owls, and the course of meteors, be around me. Let the strength of the angry blast bear me on its wings; and let the spirits of the wind hum their tales of woe in my ear.

Come forth from thy narrow dwelling in the land of graves, thou beam that was lovely. Why didst thou retire in the midst of thy blooming years, like the midnight star, that rushes behind a dark cloud? The mariners home is near its bed in the western waves. His eager eyes search for it in vain among the boisterous

boisterous billows, and blustering blasts of stormy night; but he finds it not.

Why dost thou pour the beams of thy kindness around me, bright queen of night? The friendship of thy smiles brings no joy to me. More welcome are the frowns of grizzly ghosts, the tremendous voice of bursting clouds, or the surly aspect of the wrathful storm! Away with thy glaring light, insulting moon! Hide thyself among the dark folds of nightly clouds. Never shall your smiles call forth Sulvina from the hall: Never shall your silent beams dance round her graceful shadow. The form of her who was lovely shall no more wander along the rustling heath.

The meeting of warriors is in the hall of Morauld; but the voice of mirth is not there. No white fingers are seen among the trembling strings. Mute is the harp. Loud are the sighs. What eye can refuse a tear to the lovely!

A cloud has darkened the valley at noon. The sun-beam of my joy is set, no more to return. My eyes shall never more behold its coming

coming forth from the back of the eastern hill.

Then, come, raven-haired night! with all thy black clouds. Spread thy drousy wings over the inhabitants of the forest; and let the tenants of the cottage pursue their blissful dreams among the visionary mountains that rise near the couch of their slumbers:—But talk not of sleep to me, gloomy night; My breast is the house of woe. Tho' thou rulest in darkness over the children of nature, I regard thee not. Wilt thou thyself rest, when the all-lightening sun shakes his white locks in the east: Wilt thou presume to combat the coming forth of his beauty?—No: Thou fliest in haste with thy gathered clouds; and the wretched only mourn thy departure.

Where is the course of thy journey, black cloud? Rush in haste from thy dwelling in the sky. Bring thy hundred ghosts among the dark folds of thy misty garments. Let the bending oaks and the falling rocks proclaim thy approach. Bear me on the wings of thy strength: Bear me over boisterous seas, to distant isles, where the souls of the lovely rejoice before the sun-beams of eternal day.

Do thou, Sulvina, meet me with the sweetest of thy smiles. Stretch forth thy white hand from the soft robes of thy misty cloud. Look on me in kindness; and, let the mildest beams of thy sparkling eyes fly round me like the breath of summer. Be the pillar of my wandering steps to the isle of peace.—Let me taste thy friendship in a land unknown.

ORAN-MOLLA*.

NO joy is mine in the absence of the maid of love. The white bosoms of a hundred virgins meet the sun-beams on the banks of Cormic: But thy equal, matchless maid of the rolling eye! is not there. Thy smiles are

---

* Oran-Molla, *a song of praise*—It was to this poem that the music was first composed, which, in the end of the last century, became well known in the low countries by the name of Killicranky. Some other pieces in this collection are set to music, which the Lowlanders consider as originally their own, and which the partiality of some, and the ignorance of others, have ascribed to the invention of an Italian. This makes it more than probable, that most of the Scots tunes have been composed by the Celtic bards, and entirely overthrows that ridiculous opinion, which has lately prevailed, that the best of them were done by the unfortunate

are as the glances of the fire of brightness, when he rides in meridian splendor over the mountains. Thy words as the voice of many harps, when the songs of bards are heard, and their fingers travel among the trembling strings.

Thou art distant far, maid of Cormic! But dark mountains raise their cliffy heads between us in vain. Mine eyes shall never cease to view the image of the lovely. My thoughts shall wander round the crouding beauties that attend thee.

The eager eyes of a hundred warriors are towards the captivating charms, which adorn the swelling surface of thy rising bosom †.

X The

nate Rizzio, so late as the time of Queen Mary; who, if he did any thing, can only be allowed the merit of making a few variations, and adding second parts, which the sets that are known in the Highlands generally want. There are, however, about a dozen of the best slow tunes that have no antient poem set to them in the Galic language. If ever there were any, as most probably there has, the overwhelming waves of time have buried them in oblivion.

† The Galic reader will here perceive a want. The translator has designedly left out the warm description which

The fairest lily that shines in the forest, contends not with the sweetness of its smiles; and, when it meets the sun-beams at noon, the swan is ashamed of her downy breast, and hides it beneath the rising wave. Thy which the bard has given of 'the two white hills raising 'their soft heads on the bosom of the virgin, like two bright 'sun-beams, when, smiling, they steal thro' the mist of 'Ardven, to bless the bewildered traveller.' Tho' every sentence in the original is perfectly consistent with the most rigid rules of delicacy; yet, as the bard has described his mistress's bosom a few inches lower than the ladies are pleased to expose theirs at present, the translator shall not presume to lead the readers imagination where the delicate fair will not indulge his sight.

A bard, in the last century, mentions the cause of covering the bosom as a female imposition. I shall translate the passage, not as a fact, but merely to show what injuries the fair-sex have suffered in all ages, from the capricious humours, and suspicious dispositions of the males.

The virtuous mothers of our sires deceiv'd
No youthful hero with a cover'd breast.
When virgin-purity corrupted fled,
The slacken'd breasts confess'd the secret sin.
But their fair daughters, by the aid of art,
Affecting shame unknown to innocence,
Pretend to hide, in veil of gaudy lawn,
A bosom spotless for the nuptial bed.

Imagination

Thy delicate fingers trace not in vain the folds of the lawn. Thy needle gives birth to the spreading tree, that seems to bend beneath the load of mellow fruit *.—But stretch, lovely maid! stretch forth thy hand in kindness to me, and I shall breathe, in reality, that life which the sons of thy needle but seem to enjoy. Let the friendship of thy eyes shine around me, and I will flourish before their

Imagination wanders in the dark,
And magnifies with greed the hidden store,
Which seeming modestly hoards up with care.—
Deluded lovers! sighing for a breast,
Which conscious guilt conceals from public view!

* The ladies were the only artists in this way, among the Caledonians, as well as the Greeks, and other antient nations. Instances of this, among the latter, must be obvious to every learned reader, not to mention any of our more recent ancestors.

 And aprons set wi' mony a dyce
  Of neidil-wark se rair,
 Wove be ne hand, as ze may guefs,
  Saif that of Fairly fair.

But the *Bratach*, or standard, was the usual field in which the efforts of female genius were displayed; and there have been instances, in the knight-errant strain, of warriors falling in love with ladies, whom they had never seen, from the beautiful execution of these standards.

their beams, like the vegetable tribes that rear their tender heads beneath the kindly breath of summer.

Who shall convey to song the form of the maid who moves, matchless, over the mountains? Her smooth neck is the white bed of her golden tresses. Her flowing ringlets fall in sweet disorder over her ivory shoulders *. Soft blue eyes roll beneath a small round arch. Warriors melt before the strength of their beams!

Move on in thy majestic steps, maid of the mild-rolling eye! The blooming heath shall meet

---

* The whole of this poem has sunk to an unaccountable degree of poverty in the present translation, and this passage in a particular manner. The words *Bachlach, dualach, casbhui, &c.* which astonish the Galic reader with their energy and poetical beauties, are altogether lost, as the English contains no term capable of expressing either of them. It must be acknowledged, that this language may express any sentiment that arises in the mind; but the beauties of a poem do not often depend so much on the sentiment, as the manner of expressing it. Nothing, therefore, but the sentiment can be preserved in the translation, as the genius of the two languages is so different, and as the Galic contains some thousands of words not to be found in the English.

meet thy graceful shadow in gladness: The verdant plains shall wave their grassy locks, and smile as it passeth. Grace is in thy presence. Thy breath is as the scent of a flowery garden, when it pours its sweet odours on the wings of the breeze.

The tongue of thy songs is surrounded by the white formers of the ivory ring *. The sound of

---

* What is here translated, *white formers of the ivory ring*, stands in the original *Deud, Gealdb*; a term to which no word in the English language bears the smallest affinity. When such terms occur, the translation must undoubtedly lose all the beauties of the original.

Deud signifies a graceful assemblage of refined objects, whose perfections astonish the beholders, and excite the most agreeable sensations; a term applied by the Celtic bards to the fine set teeth of the ladies.

A few remarks on this passage will contribute to support the truth of an assertion, which the translator has formerly presumed to advance; That the Galic, even in its present uncultivated state, displays a luxuriant richness of poetical terms, incomparably superior to any of the modern languages.

The care which the ladies of our days take to have the avenue leading to their gentle stomachs adorned with a proper set of ivory centinels, leaves no room to doubt, but these

of thy voice is like the music of the wood, when the feathery tribes rejoice among the rustling leaves.

O thou these champions do great execution in the day of battle. A troop, which has so often distinguished itself in the cause of the fair, ought then by no means to be forgot, when the triumphs of their victories are rehearsing; yet poetry, which pretends to do justice to every member and minute feature of the victorious beauty, has, with unpardonable negligence, suffered the teeth to sleep without their fame, while the actions of the eyes, lips, chin, &c. are magnified by repeated eulogiums.

From this general censure, however, impartiality will compel every intelligent reader to except the Celtic bards. In their most antient poems, we meet with the most beautiful poetical terms, that the nervous exertion of rhetoric could invent, to express the symmetry, whiteness, &c of the ladies teeth. But it must be owned, that the English language will not admit of any poetical sallies on this subject, till some new terms be received. The word *teeth* is harsh, and may be used with success to describe any disgustful object, as a witch, a tyger, &c. but can never be admitted with any grace in the delineation of beauty.

Did the Galic furnish no other name for teeth than *fiuchel*, the bards would have laboured under the same disadvantage. But as *those* that grimly grin in the face of an old hagg, and *these* that sweetly smile behind the vermilion

O thou who formeſt thoſe excellencies which captivate the enraptured eyes of men! this is the work of thy hand; and we feel the ſtrength of its power *. What, then, muſt be thy own perfections, ſince the object that ſtarts into exiſtence at thy nod, is thus beautifully formed!

Hide not thy fair head in the heathy mountains, bright ſon of heaven! Lonely is my ſeat on the hill of roes. The maid of the yellow locks is diſtant far: The hall of her fathers riſes on the banks of Cormic, and many gloomy hills intervene.—But thou heareſt me not, bright-haired traveller of the ſky! Thy own courſe has been over many hills to the bed of thy reſt; and why have not I reached the dwelling of the maid?—But reach it I will, O ſun! though not with a ſpeed like thine.

Why do ye fly, ye deers, with all your ſwiftneſs over the heath? No hoſtile ſteps are mine.

No

milion lips of a youthful beauty, are certainly not ſimilar objects; why ſhould the bards, who were endued with the power of inventing, and the liberty of applying terms, give them the ſame appellation?—

* The bard appears by this exclamation to have been acquainted with the true religion.

No parent of death glitters in my hand.—My speed is towards the white arms of beauty. They are seen, like two sun-beams, in the hall of the chief of Cormic.

Raise, daughter of night! raise thy fair head in the east: Be the guide of my lonely journey over the dusky mountains.

Fall softly, thou noisy stream! Steal down thy rocks in silence. The shaggy tenants of the forest are asleep: Awake them not. The hunter sits far distant from his home. The gleam of half-extinguished oaks is before him: Two faithful dogs are his shield behind. He slumbers by times on the heath; then wakes, and waits with impatience the first smiles of the morning.

When shall the hall of Cormic rear its lofty head before me?—Travel softly on your airy wings, ye winds that approach it! The white armed daughter of beauty is in the midst of her slumbers. Blow kindly, O breath of night! on the chambers of her rest; this is the season of her dreams.—Perhaps my image is seen among the children of her sleep.—Son of fancy, speak softly to the maid. Tell her my sighs are

are loud on the mountains: My groans are frequent on the hill of winds. My hounds look mournfully in my face, and wonder at the cause. They howl at my feet, and turn their wishful eyes by times to the hill of deers.— But ye look in vain, ye pursuers of the wind! the chace has no charms for me. The maid of the breast of snow is distant far, and no joy meets me on the mountains.

Though lonely, I wander by the stream, though mournful, my sigh mingles with the wind of the desart; the favour of thy bright eyes, fair maid, would cheer me, as the sun the hills, when he pours forth the strength of his beauty at noon, and shakes the snow from their heathy locks.

WORDS OF WOE.[*]

VOICE of the tale, move thou at the nod of grief, and let the words of woe be heard in the breath of the song.

Many have been the former stings which have pierced my wounded breast. These have increased the paleness of my drooping face, and thinned the ringlets of my falling hair. But other hardships appear now as nothing, and former miseries vanish before the present blow.——

Mournful are the feelings of my wounded breast. Son of the stranger! thy tear would fall,

---

[*] This poem is the composition of a lady on the death of her husband, and has been much admired in the original. Some of the best pieces in the Galic, both in the pastoral and elegiac strain, have been the productions of the fair-sex.

fall, couldst thou behold them. The mighty have fallen by the arm of death: The sword of affliction has pierced my heart. My tears bathe not the memory of the feeble. Grace and greatness were in the steps of him whose fall I mourn. He who was high among surrounding chiefs, is now the humble tenant of the peaceful grave. In vain I search for my hunter among his rocks and his woods: In vain I raise my voice among the hills of his chace. Echo answers; but he is silent. His dogs also pursue his former footsteps; but they return without him. Early in the morning they visit the chambers of his sleep; but he is not there.—I cannot ease your grief, faithful sons of swiftness! but I will join your mourning. My tears will be seen: Your moans will be heard. The stranger as he passeth will ask the cause. The tongue of information will answer, 'Because the mighty are low:'—Because the chief of Ascar is lonely in the gloomy tomb. His wife and hounds mourn his fall. All day they shun the light: The windows of the hall are shut. No open door is there to receive the traveller as he passeth; otherwise

the

the hand of invitation and the shell of friendship * had been held forth to thee, and thou hadst departed no stranger to the joys of the feast.—No wonder that the voice of woe is heard; for the chief that is low was mighty. He was fierce in the battle : He was swift in the chace : He was mild at the feast.'

Stop—son of the feeble voice! Who art thou that attempts to speak the deeds of the chief?

* The moderns are divided in their conjectures concerning the materials from which the antient Caledonians extracted the liquors which they drank out of the shells so often mentioned in their poetry. This liquor does not appear to have been strong; for we never hear of any person being intoxicate by it. According to the best accounts, there were three kinds of it. The simplest and most ordinary drink was extracted from a delicate kind of heath, known at present by the name of *French heath*; the next in quality from *juniper berries*, and their wine from the *birch*. The two last are used at present; but it is said there was a secret method of extracting ale from the heath, which is now altogether lost. The loss of this supposed secret, however, seems to have been occasioned by no other cause than the invention of malt liquor; and our moderate ancestors might have been perfectly happy with an entertainment, which our more refined palates would by no means relish.

chief? Have not I heard the secret feelings of his breast, when the words of the valiant came from his mouth?—Yet I am silent. Didst thou know the hero better than I; or is thy tongue the parent of more piercing words? Thine eyes have never shed the tears of anguish:—Thy sigh has never issued from a wounded heart.

Visage of danger! display not thy threatening brows on our mountains: He who was first to meet thee is low. The sword of the valiant is here; but where is the arm of strength?—Son of the little soul unsheath it not. Let not the sword of the mighty meet disgrace in the hands of the feeble; lest the warrior of the distant land should carry it to the hall of his fathers, and say to the maid of his love, ‘ Feel the grist of the handle, and the length of the blade.—Strong was the arm of him who grasped the parent of death; but he sank before me.’—Maid of the distant land believe it not.——

O land of ghosts! residence of every friend of mine! is there no room in your nightly chambers for me?—O chief of Ascar! thy

hall

hall has often given rest to the weary; and will thy narrow dwelling refuse to admit the wife of thy youth?—she who was wont to rejoice when the departing sun saluted the western hill; because her hunter returned at night. He returned in the strength of his beauty. His panting hounds came before; his loaded followers behind. She who waited thy coming at Crayemore, whose breast glowed at thy approach, calls:—Wilt thou not hear.—Speak, ye tenants of the grave! Your cries will be sweet unto me. The husband of my youth, the father of my children, is amongst you; he will protect me.—But no children are mine. They also walk before the moon without a shadow *.—Why so merciless to me, O grave! Thou hast wained from me the affections of those whom my breast has suckled; and wilt thou not permit them to answer me in kindness?

Chief

---

* The antients were perfectly convinced, that, although the ghosts of deceased persons wandered abroad, their bodies still remained in the grave. With very good reason, therefore, they concluded, that, where there was no substance, there could be no shadow.

Chief of Afcar!—thou who waſt great among the mighty, wilt thou not hear?—Other ghoſts roam abroad in the feaſon of darkneſs: The fons of the feeble fly in haſte; but I fly not thee. Thy grim ghoſt has no terrors for me. I fearch for thee among the dim ſhades of night; but I cannot find thee. The whirlwind is heard as it paſſeth; but thy voice is not there. The full orbed moon is in the eaſt: The poliſhed furface of the lake glitters below. Smooth are her ſteps along the half-darkened arch.—But thou ſmileſt in vain, daughter of night! The children of the den ſleep, regardleſs of thy beams. The fons of the cottage alſo purſue their peaceful dreams! No ſhadow moves before thee, but the wretched Leſbana. She mourns the fall of her huſband. Her voice is heard among the clouds of night; but he hears her not. She inquires for her hunter; but the fons of the rock return her own words for anſwer.—

O thou moon! to whom the trembling ſtars nod in obedience in the feafon of ſleep; thou haſt often travelled thy journey through the ſky.

sky. The wretched have often mourned before thee; and thou hast poured forth thy light on the mountains to comfort them. Thou permittest the inhabitants of the tomb to come forth, and leave their shadows behind. Thou shuttest the eyes of the children of day in sleep, and the hills are left free to the tenants of the grave. Why then are they not abroad?—Is my tear not big? do they not see it? Is my sigh not loud? do they not hear it?—Why then do they not answer to the voice of my grief?

Spouse of my youth! shall I taste the sweets of sleep, while the rude breath of night dashes against thy tomb in the land of graves?—No, surly blast! thou shalt not tell in other lands, that thou rushed over the tomb of the mighty, and that no soft locks rose on thy wings as thou passed. The dwelling of the hero, though narrow, shall not be unmarked. The sons of the stranger will view the stone of his fame in the season of the sun. When the course of the moon is abroad, Lesbana will mourn at his tomb. No cloud shall roll without a sigh:

No

No blaſt ſhall paſs without a portion of her falling hair. The virgins will ſeize it, and cry, ' Whence is thy journey of woe, ſoft-waving lock!'

Pleaſant art thou to Leſbana, as thou wandereſt from cloud to cloud, broad-faced ruler of the night! Sweet is thy aſpect as thou lookeſt forth in all the mildneſs of thy beauty, when the ſmile of joy is on both thy cheeks. The twinkling ſtars diminiſh in thy preſence, and ſhrink by times behind the covert of their miſty clouds.

But raiſe not the voice of thy mirth in the eaſt, fair-haired morning! Shake not the ringlets of thy beauty before me. Go to her who has loſt no lover, who comes forth from the hall when night ſpreads her duſky wing over the mountains. Her ſeat is beneath the ruſtling of an oak. Her variegated garment flutters in the blaſt: She gathers her ſcattered locks from the wind. Earneſt is the rolling of two blue ſtars below her ſoft brows. Her white arm is the pillar of her leaning cheek. She looks with expectation's eye to the hill of the chace.

Often may the return of thy hunter bless thy soft eyes, daughter of joy! But never shall a beam of mirth smile on the cheek of Lesbana. Her locks shall travel on many winds. A blast shall soon mix her with the dust. A stranger will raise the tomb of her who had no son, whose hunter sank by the arm of death.—Every virgin that passeth will give a stone *. Often will the cry be heard, 'Peace round the tomb of the mournful!'

---

* It is a custom at this day among the Highlanders, as they pass, to throw a stone into a *cairn*, which is always made at the place where any particular misfortune or death has happened. By this means, these monuments, instead of diminishing, always increase; and several very large ones are to be seen in different parts of Scotland.

THE

APPROACH of SUMMER.

MY wandering fancy returned from the pursuit of visions, as the enlightened vale proclaimed the approach of the sun. I started from the inactive couch of repose. The crystal dew trembled upon the bosom of the yielding grass along the reclining surface of the pregnant plain. The sweet voice of the pipe saluted my ear, and the aged rocks returned their approbation of the harmonious notes.

† This poem was composed by a gentleman of universal knowledge, about forty years ago. He attempted, in other compositions, to introduce the beauties of the Greek and Roman poets into the Galic language. But, as he entered too warmly into the political controversy of his time, his works, in general, must be excluded from a translation. The reader, from this specimen, however will readily perceive the superiority of native genius, unassisted by any other qualification, over the self-sufficient knowledge of literature, and the little embellishments of art.

The birch sent forth infant branches thro' the opening jaws of the disjointed rock. The blue mist of the morning leaned on the bushes which adorned the brow of the hill; but it fled the approach of the ascending sun, whose friendly beams smiled upon the half formed daughter of the feeble twig.

Sweet is the beauty which adorns thy spreading leaves, smiling primrose of the grateful hue! Thou art the most courageous warrior of the vegetable race. While other flowers are buried in the bosom of the earth, faint-hearted sons of the tender roots, thy steps are forward to combat the breath of the still-subsisting cold. Clothed in the armour of thy beauty, thou art the earliest jewel that adorns the brow of the infant spring.

The spreading roots of trees extend their pasture through the hidden bowels of the earth, in search of enriching draughts to increase the strength of the stately plant. With impartial justice, the trunk destributes the ascending juice through each twisting vein. Her grateful offspring spread the leafy garments round the parent of their wealth;
and

and the thrush, enfolded in their skirts, pours forth the harmonious song in the bosom of the morning. Every member of the vocal concert flies to the collecting branches of the wood. Their little breasts are flushed with joy at the approaching light. A hundred voices from the thickest thorn, proclaim the welcome of the infant day. The voice of the little wren is mingled in the general sound; and the red-breasted songster is heard on the outmost verge of the projecting branch.

O glorious fountain of light! bright daughter of the east, welcome is thy northward journey to the wishing eyes of nature and her sons. The hills, robbed by the surly breath of winter of the garments with which thou lately clothed them, spread forth their shivering bosoms before thee with seeming complaints, and solicit thy chearing aid to heal the wounds of the frosty blast.—They petition not in vain. The darting arrows of thy beams defeat the efforts of the retiring cold.

The collecting veins of the rill swell with the rapid descent of the melting snow. And, by thy majestic presence, every gloom which
frowned

frowned on the surface of the earth, trembling, disappears. Fly, congealing foe of increase; the united sons of nature shall assemble to rejoice in your absence; the little daisies, eager to partake of the smiles of summer, start from behind their green curtain, and present themselves clad in golden charms of infant purity. Early herbs are clothed in the livery of the spring; and the roving bee, bewildered in choice, tastes the riches of every flower, and joyfully hums amidst surrounding wealth.

The admiring eyes of the traveller are lost among the crouding beauties of the variegated plains; and his ears are ravished with the voice of harmony and love. The joys of nature still increase; for now the ascending sun, with uniform pace, has gained the summit of the azure arch, and drives the shadow of the high-erected hills from the enlightened bottom of the hollow glens. The feathered tenant of the bush, with joy beholds the welcome change, and pours the melodious offspring of his warbling throat on the bosom of expanded light. No cloud of surly aspect travels on the top of the mountains, to intercept

cept the favours of the bountiful sun, or silence the music of the choral bands.

The words of paternal love are in the breath of the herds, as they disperse in search of the flowery pasture. The green-covered plains round the thickest grove, smile under their increasing wealth, and invite the straggling flocks to taste the richness of their luxuriant crop.

Sweet are the words of thy music, and beautiful the varying garment of thy pride, lovely warbler of the quick-moving eye! Thy seat is on the loftiest branch of the towering oak of many years, whose strong-jointed trunk has long withstood the breath of the blustering blast. Her dwelling is not on the top of the barren hill: She collects the riches of her strength by the side of the fertile stream, on the brow of the verdant vale.

The animating breath of the sun calls forth a thousand herbs from the prolific womb of the pregnant plain; opening flowers are surrounded by leaves projecting from the bending stalk; and every species of the vegetable tribe shines in its gayest garments along the joyful glen. Sweet is the scent of the
flowery

flowery plain which furrounds the bottom of the erected rock; the fpreading rofes fhake their leaves upon the waving ftalk before the friendly breeze; with joy they tafte the welcome embrace. But their nod is on the top of a more extended ftalk, whofe moifty dwelling is on the fertile bofom of the fruitful mead.

The gentle lily, foft emblem of virgin purity, with unaffected grace, adorns the hollow of the mountains that gradually form the curve along the twifting verge of the defcending rill. Her decent robes are not the work of oftentatious gaudy fingers; her modeft looks are from the pale garments of the white leaf, near the fhade of the rifing bufh, where the morning often finds the roe, ere he ftarts from his couch of reft.

Now the herds repair to the well-known fold, to have their udders eafed of the milky load. Their voice is joined with the fhepherd's pipe to quicken the fteps of the dairy nymphs: Welcome are their prefence to the expecting flocks, who liften attentive to the quivering fong.

Darting through the yielding ftream, the ftately falmon cleaves with eafe a paffage. His
fpeed

speed is from the strength of his finny wings, as he pursues the course of the unwary fly, whose shortened life perishes within his opening jaws. The son of the flood springs with joy along the liquid plains; the variegated scales of his sparkling side and silver wings, wantonly sport along the crystal stream.

Flushed with the joys of conjugal love, the wood-cock, from the spreading tree, takes his airy flight to the less masculine cover of the heathy plain; with watchful looks he rears his waving crest above the slender branches of the heath; his steps are in search of the coy charmer of his breast, whose half-inviting distant notes he eagerly pursues with joyful flight; with majestic grace he shakes the varying colour of his swelling pride, and solicits the friendly glances of the female eye, while the spreading wing invites her to the warm embrace. Fly not the arms of thy lover, daughter of the heath; this is the nuptial season of the feathered tribe: Every tender pair taste the pleasures of love in the heathy locks of the surrounding hills. The joys of nature, without interruption, be thy portion, sprightly daughter of the nimble eye! thy grateful lover will remain faithful to the charmer of his breaſt; he will yet provide thee food, and cheer thy heart with melodious notes from the diſtant tree, when thou ſpreadeſt thy motherly wings o'er the tenants of the neſt; and, with the animating kindneſs of thy ſpeckled boſom, warm into exiſtence a feeble crew, the feathered ſons of the ſhell.

Thus, fed by the liberal hand of nature, paſs ye the day, ſweet tuned warblers, until the dark cloud of night from the eaſt prepares to ſupplant the departing light. Then let the children of the wood ſtrain every muſcle, and pour forth the choice offspring of their throats, to ſolicit the ſpeedy return of departing light.

The theme ceaſed; let ſilence enſue; and, let the little buſhes open their hoſpitable gates to receive their nightly gueſts.

THE
ANTIENT CHIEF.*

HAPPY the bard who sung in former days,
   When Albin heard with joy her heroes praise;
When her sons rush'd with courage to the fields,
Where echoing rocks proclaim'd the noise of shields.
Her warrior, when the sheath receiv'd his sword,
Tasted each blessing which its edge secur'd.
His chief was ruler only to defend
The weak from insults, and make tyrants bend;
                              To

---

* This poem, a translation of which appeared some time ago in a periodical publication, was composed by CALLUM RUADH, a bard still alive in the Highlands, in the time of the late emigration to America. It is here inserted, not so much on account of its merit, as to show the present taste of the Highland poetry, and to represent the hardships which many of the inhabitants of that country suffer from the tyrannical *viceroys* of some chiefs.

To cheer the aged and inftruct the young,
To hear each conteft and redrefs each wrong.
At his tribunal open were the laws,
No fubftitute was hir'd to plead the caufe;
A guardian to his clan he pafs'd his days,
The firft in danger, but the laft in eafe.
His arm fecur'd his people in the field,
The feeble refted fafe behind his fhield;
Beneath his hand the weak did never fall;
The fons of want found plenty in his hall;
The ftranger there might uninvited come,
And tafte each comfort which he left at home:
Free to the traveller was the daily feaft,
And the foe always perifh'd in the gueft.

 Thrice happy bards who fung of chiefs like thefe!
Your works have always met deferved praife;
The grateful fons of Gael have nurs'd your fame,
And diftant ages will rever your name:
Each eye fhall foften at your lofty fong,
Which ne'er fhall fink but with the Galic tongue *.

Not

---

* The Galic is the only name the Highlanders have for their own language. Their neighbours in the fouth, however, have not been idle in inventing others, as *Irifh* and *Erfe*. Even the Highlanders themfelves, when they talk

Not so the guilty chief of modern days,
Unknown to virtue, and inur'd to ease;
          He,

of it in the low countries, distinguish it by the appellation by which it is best understood there.

The Rev. Mr Whitaker, whose assertions I have formerly presumed to combat, concludes this to be a sufficient demonstration that the Scots are of Irish extraction. As this affair is of some consequence in a controverted point of history, the reader will not, perhaps, be displeased to see the authorities on which this reverend historian proceeds, examined. ' The Caledonians, who were reduced by the Scots of Er-in, or Ireland, having adopted the appellation of their conquerors; the nation and the country being now universally denominated Scots and Scotland; the nation being expresly denominated Hibernia, as late as the 11th century, and the people the Irischery, as late as the 14th, and their dialect of the British being *invariably* entitled the Ir-ish, or Er-se, to the present moment.' *Whitaker's hist. page 292.*

So far is the language of the Highlands from ' being *invariably* entitled Ir-ish, or Er-se,' at this, or any former period, that not one instance can be found of its having ever been termed by either of these names by the natives, until they come abroad, and learn it from strangers. But this extract is supported by a quotation from a respectable author of the last century, and has the following note.

' Irwin in his hist. Scot. nomenclatura, 1682, p. 6. says,
' Our isle-men and Highlanders are very oft named Hi-
                     berni

He, void of pity, hears the wretched moan,
And human nature give a gen'ral groan.—

With

berni by ſtrangers;—and, *at this day*, the Engliſh and our lowlanders call and count them Iriſh.'

When Mr Whitaker entered on the preſent controverſy with James Macpherſon, Eſq; he ſet out with profeſſions of candour, which could not fail of anticipating the favourable opinion of every reader of liberal ſentiments. His expreſſions are beautiful, and ſeem to bear the genuine marks of ſincerity.—' Diſdaining the little artifices of controverſy, too honourable, I hope, to create the faults that I cannot find, and too candid, I truſt, to urge ſtrongly the mere failings of humanity,' &c.

Can we imagine the author of ſentiments which do honour to human nature, capable of forgetting that reſpect due to himſelf, and proſtituting his ſuperior talents, by committing the moſt deſpicable piece of forgery that ever diſgraced the meaneſt controverſy. Candour and humanity forbid the ungenerous ſuſpicion; but juſtice calls aloud on the auſterity of truth, and confirms the fact.

From the following genuine quotation from the paſſage referred to, the reader will ſee what juſtice Mr Whitaker has done to his authority, and, from thence, may perceive what degree of credit is due to his moſt poſitive aſſertions.

' *Albinenſis Scotia, et Albinenſes Scoti*, the country of *Albin*, and the *Scots* that poſſeſs it in Britain: For *Ireland* was never called *Scotia*, nor its inhabitants *Scoti-Hibernenſes*; though ſome *ſtrangers* have been over-eaſy to believe the monkiſh ridiculous fable of the

Iriſh,

With grief he loads the wretched sons of care,
And thousands starve that he may sumptuous
fare.
While I'm condemn'd to sing of chiefs like
these,
My works shall neither meet nor merit praise:
                                              No

Irish, who affirm that *Ireland* was called *Scotia Major*, and they were called *Scoti Hibernenses*. The ground of the mistake was, That they thought both people might be as well called *Scots*, as (Gaelick) *Galœci*. The truth is, the *Irish* are never called *Scots* in any authentic author. But our Isle-men and Highlanders are very often named Hiberni by strangers; both from their west situation, from their original, being come of the same *Gaelicks* in *Spain*, and from their language, and divers of their customs, all common with the Irish. And, at this day, the *English* and our *lowlanders*, call and count them *Irish*, for the foresaid reasons.' *Irwin's hist. Scot. Nomencl.* p. 6.

From *faults* thus *created*, and from authorities thus perverted, does the reverend author conclude his *extended* remarks, in the loftiest strain of encomiums on his own abilities, that ever issued from a pen, elevated to an uncommon degree by the complimenting voice of self-approbation. Had Mr Whitaker avoided all reference to the Celtic language, these eulogiums to his own talents had been less liable to censure. In other respects, he displays the ingenuity of a penetrating critic, and every where discovers an extensive knowledge of antient history.

No bard shall sound them on the trembling string,
My words shall perish, and the names I sing.
  In vain, alas! I tempt the lyric art,
With pointless words that reach not to the heart:
How shall I virtues which exist not, draw,
Or sing of greatness which I never saw?
Weak are my words; for fate has cast my birth
In the dull evening of the day of worth:
But stories tell that light did once prevail,
And the sweet songs of bards confirm the tale;
These say that nature smil'd with joy at noon,
When rays came darting from the glorious sun:
But I too long in chaos did remain,
And now, alas! I trace his steps in vain;
Crouds who have seen him cry *the light divine*,
But tho' some eyes were bleft, they were not mine;
Yon western hill has snatch'd him from my sight,
And my soul trembles at th' approach of night;
Concealing darkness spreads her awful gloom,
And music's words are hast'ning to their tomb:
The language of the glens is left for death,
While jargon issues from the south born breath;
The growling accents * form'd by rules of art,
Reach not the soul, nor pierce into the heart.
                                      The

---

* The bard was provoked to pronounce this severe cen-
                                                 sure

The moon with English rhetoric in her train,
Strives to supplant the setting sun in vain:
                                          But

sure on the English language, from the liberty with which
a gentleman from the south had once, in his presence,
treated the Galic. He asserted, that it was an unintelligible jargon, which ought not to be permitted in a civilized
nation. This assertion was translated to the bard, who
gave his opinion of the English much in the same terms;
and both parties continued to express a hearty contempt
for what neither of them understood.

  This, it is hoped, would be a sufficient apology for the
austerity of the bard, had not I myself been guilty of an
equal piece of rudeness in the preceding notes; and frequently accused the English language of being incapable to
admit a multiplicity of beauties contained in the originals
of these poems. Therefore, before I conclude this volume, it is reasonable I should produce more particular instances in support of these assertions. An examination of
a passage, even of a modern composition, will illustrate
this. It is taken from the works of a bard in the last century, when the office of bard and piper were united in one
person.

  'Sa mhaduinn aig eiridh le'r miolchoin,
   Gu muirneach, maiseach, gasda, gniomhach,
   Lubach, leacach, glacach, sgiamhach,
   Carach, cabrach, enagach, fiamhach.
  'Nam da'n ghrein dol air a huisinn,
   Gu fuilteach, reubach, gleusda, gunnach,

But feeble were her rays and dim she shone,
Equal in nought but bulk to him that's gone.
Yet absent brightness she insulting dares,
And thinks she's great among the twinkling stars:
These fled the presence of the fire of light;
Tho' now they blaze behind the queen of night.
  So fled oppression once the glens of mirth,
When ev'ry day gave new-born pleasures birth.

Small

> Snapach, armach, calgach, ullamh,
> Riachach, marbhach, tarbhach, giullach.

In the first paragraph, the bard describes a chief and his party going out to the hunting in the morning. This description is contained in twelve beautiful and comprehensive terms in the three last lines, not one of which can be literally translated. Each of them contains a complete piece of imagery, and would require a paragraph to express it in English.

Having sent them to the field with all the accomplishments which the most fertile fancy could suggest, or the most strenuous exertion of rhetoric express, he leaves the imagination to form to itself the actions of the day, and proceeds immediately to describe their return in the evening, with the spoils of the chace, 'when the sun leans on his elbow.' This is also done in twelve descriptive terms; the two first of which, representing the streaming blood and gaping wounds of the venison, may be translated literally; the rest are, like the other twelve, altogether inimitable.

THE ANTIENT CHIEF.

Small was the tribute which the chieftain drew,
Yet many were his flocks, his wants were few;
His open table waited on the gueſt,
Nor falted thouſands to provide the feaſt;
He liv'd not on the ſons of labour's ſpoil,
Themſelves enjoy'd the offspring of their toil,
His arm gave aid, his face did joy inſpire,
But never—never quench'd the peaſant's fire.
  So rul'd the virtuous *Caledonian* ſage
In days which moderns term a barbarous age,
In ſelf-defence he drew the bloody dart;
No mercenary prieſt corrupt his heart.
Religious murder had not yet begun,
Nor ſuperſtition half mankind undone:
The gifts of nature to her ſons were free;
Thro' gratitude, not fear, man bent the knee.
  Oh happy days! which will no more return;
Thy vaniſh'd brightneſs I'll with anguiſh mourn.
No more my harp ſhall tremble in the hall,
Since I have liv'd to ſee my country fall;
Her ſmoakleſs village and unpeopl'd glens,
Point out the tyranny which holds her reins;
The chief whoſe province 'twas to grant relief,
Is the black cauſe of every piercing grief.
Oh ſons of pride! what havock have you wrought!
What ruin on your wretched country brought!

You've ftab'd the bofom of a tott'ring ftate,
And broke that fword whofe edge has made you
	great;
Forc'd *Albin's* fons to quit their native land,
And feek protection from a favage band;
Driv'n by fome chiefs of little foul from home,
To fink in boift'rous waves, or find a tomb.

 So when with flinty fparks the fire of death
Blows the hot bullet from his fmoaky breath,
The feeding ftag comes tottering to the ground,
And echoing hills return the lofty found;
The painful ftings begin to ftop his breath,
His half-chew'd mouthful drops upon the heath;
The hated note alarms the fwift-foot train,
Who ftretch each nerve to gain the diftent glen.
The many horned foreheads cleave the wind;
With rapid fpeed the hills fly back behind.

 So fly the fons of *Gael* oppreffion's rod,
So fhun the paths that pale-fac'd tyrants trode.
Gone are our warriors, barren are our vales,
Yet I am left to tell thefe woeful tales;
To fing of thofe who under tyrants bend,
And mourn the evils which I cannot mend.

www.ingramcontent.com/pod-product-compliance
Lightning Source LLC
Chambersburg PA
CBHW020926230426
43666CB00008B/1589